IRISH LEGAL HISTORY SOCIETY

The Sir Anthony Hart Doctoral Paper Prize

This volume was presented to

Ian King

on the occasion

of

The 2022 British Legal History Conference

hosted by

Queen's University Belfast
and
The Irish Legal History Society

8 July, 2022
President

AN ISLAND'S LAW

IN THIS SERIES*

1. Daire Hogan and W.N. Osborough (eds), *Brehons, serjeants and attorneys: studies in the history of the Irish legal profession* (1990)
2. Colum Kenny, *King's Inns and the kingdom of Ireland: the Irish 'inn of court', 1541–1800* (1992)
3. Jon G. Crawford, *Anglicizing the government of Ireland: the Irish privy council and the expansion of Tudor rule, 1556–1578* (1993)
4. W.N. Osborough (ed.), *Explorations in law and history: Irish Legal History Society discourses, 1988–1994* (1995)
5. W.N. Osborough, *Law and the emergence of modern Dublin: a litigation topography for a capital city* (1996)
6. Colum Kenny, *Tristram Kennedy and the revival of Irish legal training, 1835–1885* (1996)
7. Brian Griffin, *The Bulkies: police and crime in Belfast, 1800–1865* (1997)
8. Éanna Hickey, *Irish law and lawyers in modern folk tradition* (1999)
9. A.R. Hart, *A history of the king's serjeants at law in Ireland: honour rather than advantage?* (2000)
10. D.S. Greer and N.M. Dawson (eds), *Mysteries and solutions in Irish legal history: Irish Legal History Society discourses and other papers, 1996–1999* (2000)
11. Colum Kenny, *King's Inns and the battle of the books, 1972: cultural controversy at a Dublin library* (2002)
12. Desmond Greer and James W. Nicolson, *The factory acts in Ireland, 1802–1914* (2003)
13. Mary Kotsonouris, *The winding-up of the Dáil courts, 1922–1925: an obvious duty* (2004)
14. Paul Brand, Kevin Costello and W.N. Osborough (eds), *Adventures of the law: proceedings of the 16th British Legal History Conference, Dublin 2003* (2005)
15. Jon G. Crawford, *A star chamber court in Ireland: the court of castle chamber, 1571–1641* (2005)
16. A.P. Quinn, *Wigs and guns: Irish barristers and the Great War* (2006)
17. N.M. Dawson (ed.), *Reflections on law and history: Irish Legal History Society discourses and other papers, 2000–2005* (2006)
18. James Kelly, *Poynings' Law and the making of law in Ireland, 1660–1800* (2007)
19. W.E. Vaughan, *Murder trials in Ireland, 1836–1914* (2009)
20. Kevin Costello, *The Court of Admiralty of Ireland, 1575–1893* (2011)
21. W.N. Osborough, *An island's law: a bibliographical guide to Ireland's legal past* (2013)

ALSO AVAILABLE

The Irish Legal History Society (1989)

*Volumes 1–7 are published by Irish Academic Press.

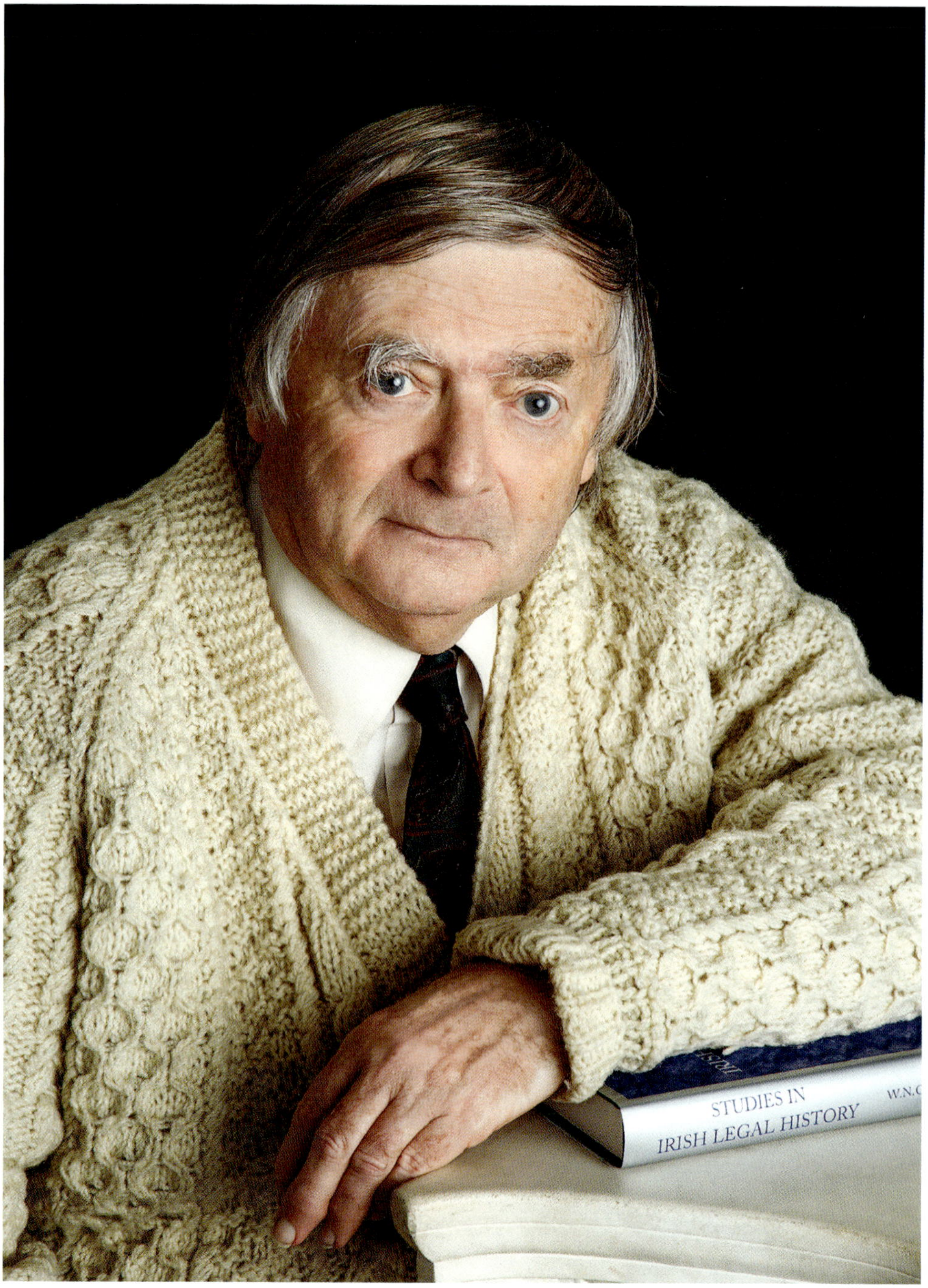
STUDIES IN
IRISH LEGAL HISTORY

An Island's Law

A Bibliographical Guide to Ireland's Legal Past

W.N. OSBOROUGH

FOUR COURTS PRESS
in association with
THE IRISH LEGAL HISTORY SOCIETY

Typeset in 11pt on 13.5pt EhrhardtMtPro by
Carrigboy Typesetting Services for
FOUR COURTS PRESS LTD
7 Malpas Street, Dublin 8, Ireland
www.fourcourtspress.ie
and in North America for
FOUR COURTS PRESS
c/o ISBS, 920 N.E. 58th Avenue, Suite 300, Portland, OR 97213.

© W.N. Osborough 2013

A catalogue record for this title is available
from the British Library.

ISBN 978–1–84682–416–6

All rights reserved.
Without limiting the rights under copyright
reserved alone, no part of this publication may be
reproduced, stored in or introduced into a retrieval system,
or transmitted, in any form or by any means (electronic, mechanical,
photocopying, recording or otherwise), without the prior
written permission of both the copyright owner and
publisher of this book.

Printed in England,
by Antony Rowe Ltd, Chippenham, Wilts.

Contents

FOREWORD	7
PREFACE	9
ABBREVIATIONS	12

1. Recent writing on Irish legal history (1986) — 13
   - 1.1 Introduction — 13
   - 1.2 Chronological surveys — 15
   - 1.3 Constitutional history — 19
   - 1.4 The courts of law — 23
   - 1.5 Substantive law — 27
   - 1.6 Public administration — 29
   - 1.7 Biography — 30
   - 1.8 The profession, education and publishing — 31
   - 1.9 Conclusion — 33

2. Recent writing on Irish legal history (2008) — 35
   - 2.1 Introduction — 35
   - 2.2 General narratives — 35
   - 2.3 Constitutional developments — 38
   - 2.4 The courts — 42
   - 2.5 Substantive law — 45
     - *2.5.1 Ecclesiastical law* — 45
     - *2.5.2 Law of property* — 46
     - *2.5.3 Labour law* — 48
     - *2.5.4 Commercial law* — 49
     - *2.5.5 Procedure and evidence* — 49
   - 2.6 Administration of criminal justice — 50
   - 2.7 The legal profession — 55
   - 2.8 Judicial biography — 59
   - 2.9 Courthouses — 62
   - 2.10 Legal writing and publishing — 62
   - 2.11 Conclusion — 64
   - 2.12 Addenda — 65

3.	Further writing on Irish legal history (2012)	66
	3.1 Early Irish law	66
	3.2 Medieval Ireland	69
	3.3 The post-medieval legal system in the common law dispensation	70
	3.4 Constitutional law	74
	3.5 Legislation	78
	3.6 The courts	79
	3.7 Local government	81
	3.8 Land use and land law	82
	3.9 Civil liability	83
	3.10 Commercial law	84
	3.11 Labour law	84
	3.12 Charities law	85
	3.13 Crime and criminal justice	85
	3.14 The judiciary	89
	3.15 Legal profession	90
	3.16 Courthouses	93
	3.17 Law reporting	93
	3.18 An Epilogue	94

THE INAUGURATION OF THE IRISH LEGAL HISTORY
   SOCIETY   96

A TRIBUTE TO NIAL   101

INDEX OF AUTHORS   105

GENERAL INDEX   133

THE IRISH LEGAL HISTORY SOCIETY   143

Foreword

One of Professor Nial Osborough's many services to Irish legal history scholarship has been the undertaking of periodic surveys of recent writing in that area. Two such surveys were published in the German *Journal of Modern Legal History (Zeitschrift für Neuere Rechtsgeschichte*, or *ZNR)* in 1986 and 2008.[1] It occurred to us that these papers should be more widely known and that, if they were brought together with an update on Irish legal history publications since 2008, they would make a very valuable resource for others working in the field. The publishers of *ZNR* have kindly agreed to the republication of Professor Osborough's papers, and we thank them. For his part, Professor Osborough enthusiastically agreed to bring his earlier work up to date to 2012. We are delighted to make this material available to members of the Society and to wider scholarly circles, in the belief that it will foster and inspire fresh endeavours of those working in the field.

The publication of this volume in the Irish Legal History Society's twenty-fifth anniversary year also gives us an opportunity to mark Professor Osborough's outstanding contribution to the Society, which he founded in 1988. Here we reproduce the text of the inaugural lecture, delivered by Nial in Dublin on 12 February 1988 in the presence of the Chief Justice of Ireland and the Lord Chief Justice of Northern Ireland. Nial has served the Society with distinction in the intervening years, and when he stepped down in 2010 as a member of the Council of the Society, we felt the loss keenly and continue to do so. But the Society continues to flourish and is in good heart, thanks in no small measure to his leadership over many years. Council members organized a dinner in his honour in May 2011, and the tribute which I paid to Nial on that occasion is also published below. Nial continues, of course, to play a vital part at meetings of the Society: long may he do so.

Norma Dawson
January 2013

---

[1] W.N. Osborough, 'Recent writing on modern Irish legal history', *ZNR*, 8 (1986), 180–94, and *ZNR*, 30 (2008), 93–116.

Shown above is a Gold Collar of SS, now in the custody of Trinity College Dublin. Such collars came to be worn by holders of high judicial office in Ireland on a regular basis from the mid-nineteenth century, but as the late Vincent Delany pointed out ((1961) 77 LQR. 169), 'there is ample pictorial evidence of the insignia having been worn in Ireland at a much earlier date'.

This particular collar, of silver gilt, was manufactured in London in 1866 to the order of Chief Justice Whiteside of the Irish Queen's Bench. It was later to come into the possession of Sir Thomas Molony Bt, the last Lord Chief Justice of Ireland and retained by him until his death in 1949. In his will Molony bequeathed the collar to Trinity College in trust 'until such time as the office of Lord Chief Justice shall be restored'.

Trinity College Dublin Silver Collection. Reproduced by kind permission from the Board of Trinity College Dublin.

Preface

The three bibliographical essays reproduced in the present volume are designed to facilitate the travails of would-be researchers into Ireland's legal past. Hopefully, their appearance together in this compact edition will in consequence receive a welcome from those who aspire to unravel the mysteries of a subject which in general terms is still relatively unexplored. There is in existence no single text that tackles Ireland's legal story from the setting down of the early Irish law tracts up to the twentieth century – a lacuna that well illustrates the need for the effort to be made to recruit newcomers to this field of intellectual endeavour.

The first two essays – 'Recent writing on modern Irish legal history' (1986) and 'Recent writing on modern Irish legal history' (2008) – were commissioned by, and published in, the leading German-language legal history periodical, the *Zeitschrift für Neuere Rechtsgeschichte*. They are reprinted here with permission, and I am particularly grateful to Professor Wilhelm Brauneder of Vienna on *ZNR*'s editorial panel for his assistance in this connection.

The third essay – 'Further writing on Irish legal history' – is new, and is intended to bring bibliographical information in respect of the island's legal history up to date. The second of these bibliographical essays, at the request of the editors of the *ZNR*, ignored writings that predated the late fifteenth century. Early Irish law and the law of the medieval lordship were thus omitted from the coverage attempted. In my new third essay, an effort has been made to plug these quite serious gaps. But, as will be plain from a scrutiny of the text of this essay, I have sought principally to bring matters up to date since essay no. 2 appeared in 2008.

The text of the first two essays is reprinted here with but a modicum of minor alterations – the furnishing of complete references for a number of books and articles still in the press at the relevant time – 1986 or 2008. In the first essay, mention of 'the present century' is, of course, a reference to the twentieth, something that it is crucial for the reader of this essay to bear in mind. That this first essay may appear dated in certain other respects merits another word of caution. In 1986, the year of its publication, the malicious injuries code (see 1.5) still survived; its fortunes subsequently were set to plummet. Allusions in the same essay are sometimes made to deficiencies in published works or, more commonly, to the need for additional tasks to be carried out: allusions accompanying discussion of such topics as the penal laws, criminal justice, the legal profession and legal and judicial biography. Thankfully, a reading of the two ensuing essays will often show that these deficiencies have been rectified; alternatively, that the suggested tasks in question have, in part at least, been tackled. It is only necessary to draw attention to the publication in 2004 of the *Oxford dictionary of national biography* or that in 2009 of the 9 volumes of the *Dictionary of Irish biography* for the reader to start to grasp how any shortfall in biographical writing has begun to be eliminated. This serves as but one example.[1]

Even where particular lacunae have not been highlighted in this fashion, the reader will find that a number of later publications have superseded, or complemented, research in an earlier inventory, in the process demonstrably increasing our understanding and bidding fair to establish themselves as leading authorities in their respective fields. A listing here risks being incomplete, but it does seem appropriate to draw attention to such achievements as – Treadwell's work on the 1622 Commission; Crawford's book on Castle Chamber; Costello's book on Admiralty; Maureen Walls' collected essays on the penal laws; James Kelly's research on the later history of Poynings' Law; Vaughan's book on nineteenth-century murder trials; Hall's book on law reporting; Kotsonouris' two books on the Dáil Courts; and Hogan's text on the origins of the Irish Constitution of 1937. For early Irish law Fergus Kelly's *Guide* belongs to the same stable of classic texts as does Hand's invocation of the arrival of the common law on the island.

Several individuals of a recent generation toiling in the field of Irish legal history and whose published oeuvre feature in the ensuing inventories are no longer with us. It is a melancholy duty to note their passing: Michael Adams, Daniel Binchy, Kevin Boyle, Jim Brady,

---

1   Four essays in the forthcoming Irish Legal History Society volume, edited by Felix M. Larkin and N.M. Dawson, *Lawyers, the law and history: Irish Legal Society discourses and other papers, 2005–2011* testify to the progress it is only right to record:
    (i) James McGuire, 'Lawyers in the *Dictionary of Irish Biography*';
    (ii) Lord Carswell, 'Founding a legal system: the early judiciary of Northern Ireland';
    (iii) Hugh Geoghegan, 'The three judges of the Supreme Court of the Irish Free State, 1925–1936: their backgrounds, personalities and mindsets';
    (iv) Robert D. Marshall, 'Lieutenant W.E. Wylie KC: the soldiering lawyer of 1916'.

Philomena Connolly, Donal Cregan, Margaret Griffith, Robert Heuston, David Johnson, R.B. McDowell, Paul O'Higgins.

In the preparation of the present volume for the press, I owe a huge debt of gratitude to Sandra Maxwell. She has reset the text of the first two essays, and produced copy for the third from a holograph. Dr Robin Hickey edited the revised version of text, to which two sets of further additions came in at a late hour, which cannot have made things any easier to handle. *An island's law* includes two indexes – an Index of authors and a General index. I am grateful to Julitta Clancy for contributing both indexes, especially for the speed and efficiency with which the task was accomplished.

If, as I have indicated above, there are still too few toilers in the field of Irish legal history, that there has been an upsurge of interest in that field is surely demonstrated by the number and quality of published articles and books that have been brought out in four short years. It is a pleasure to be able to herald the achievement of all the authors concerned.

Nial Osborough
January 2013

Abbreviations

Abbreviations employed in this survey:

AJLH	*American Journal of Legal History*
Anal Hib	*Analecta Hibernica*
BJC	*British Journal of Criminology*
DULJ	*Dublin University Law Journal*
HMC	Historical Manuscripts Commission
IHS	*Irish Historical Studies*
ICLR	Irish Common Law Reports
IESH	*Irish Economic and Social History*
IJ	*Irish Jurist*
IMC	Irish Manuscripts Commission
IR CL	Irish Reports Common Law
JLAS	*Journal of the Louth Archaeological Society*
JRSAI	*Journal of the Royal Society of Antiquaries of Ireland*
NILQ	*Northern Ireland Legal Quarterly*
PRIA	Proceedings of the Royal Irish Academy
Stud Hib	*Studia Hibernica*
TRHS	Transactions of the Royal Historical Society
ZCP	Zeitschrift für Celtische Philologie

† denotes a publication of Irish Legal History Society
* denotes publication of Irish Manuscripts Commission

1

Recent writing on Irish legal history (1986)

1.1 INTRODUCTION

In 1843 the historian and antiquarian James Hardiman published an edition of the Statutes of Kilkenny 1366[1] for the recently founded Irish Archaeological Society. Like Hardiman's more renowned *History of Galway* (1820), the edition is generously supplied with footnotes. One of these reveals an appreciation, certainly uncommon at the time, of the need to encourage the study of Irish legal history. 'An historical account', Hardiman was moved to observe:

> of the rise, progress and constitution of the courts of justice, both law and equity, in Ireland, from the time of the arrival of the English, including also the Courts of Star Chamber, Wards and Liveries, Claim &c (for which there is abundance of recorded materials, if collected with care, and arranged with judgment) would form an important addition to our national history.[2]

In the course of the next hundred years a tradition of sound Irish historical scholarship was to be built up by writers of the calibre of MacNeill, Orpen, Bagwell, Dunlop, Froude and Lecky. Archival work executed by Gilbert and several others over the same period was destined to prove of equal enduring worth. It is disappointing therefore to be forced to acknowledge that James Hardiman's appeal of 1843 on behalf of Irish legal history would seem very largely to have fallen on deaf ears. Yet fortunately some qualification is warranted, for there were to be exceptions. Essays and papers from C.L. Falkiner, H.F. Berry, H. Wood, R. Thurneysen and W.J. (later Mr Justice) Johnston

---

[1] A modern text will be found conveniently in E. Curtis and R.B. McDowell (eds), *Irish historical documents, 1172–1922* (London, 1943), p. 52. This collection of material is of general utility.
[2] *Tracts relating to Ireland*, II (1843), at p. 14.

explored a diverse range of questions and can all still be read with profit today. In his *Guide to the records deposited in the Public Record Office of Ireland* (1919), which appeared shortly before the vast bulk of these records was to be destroyed at the outset of the Irish civil war of 1922–3, Wood additionally committed to print a veritable treasure-store of information on the history of the Irish legal system. Though Wood's *Guide* has not eluded criticism,[3] it remains an invaluable work of reference. Finally, in 1926 F.E. Ball published his celebrated two-volume history, *The judges of Ireland, 1221–1921*. Ball employed sources which are no longer extant, is particularly enlightening on various aspects of the seventeenth and eighteenth centuries, and the book remains likewise an indispensable thesaurus.

Nonetheless, overall, and clearly by comparison with what had been attempted elsewhere, the Irish attainment was meagre enough, a verdict endorsed by the late F.H. Newark in telling fashion in 1947. Newark had arrived ten years before as a young law lecturer at Queen's University, Belfast, and had become eager to impart something of the history of law in Ireland to his students. He recounted the frustration he experienced on discovering that there was no reliable guide to which he could turn: 'Immediately I came upon the obstacle that there was no one source from which information could come. Ireland not only awaited its Reeves or Holdsworth; it lacked even any elementary book or monograph in Irish legal history'.[4]

Newark himself set out to remedy the deficiency. The result was his 'Notes on Irish legal history' (1947), recently reprinted in: F.J. McIvor (ed.), *Elegantia juris: selected writings of F.H. Newark* (Belfast, 1973), p. 203. Newark's 'Notes' are brief, almost skeletal, and the emphasis lies unashamedly on the institutional, principally the evolution of the Irish superior courts. Complications are avoided and the law of Gaelic Ireland, undeniably part of Irish legal history prior to the seventeenth century, is all but ignored. Nevertheless, as the single general survey of Irish legal history to emerge so far, Newark's 'Notes' remain essential preliminary reading. Early chapters in A.G. Donaldson, *Some comparative aspects of Irish law* (Durham, NC, 1957) add a leavening of detail to Newark's *aperçu*.

Others too have striven to make amends. This report constitutes an account and an assessment of their combined labours. While the report

3 R.W. Dudley Edwards and M. O'Dowd, *Sources for early modern Irish history, 1534–1641* (Cambridge, 1985), p. 10.
4 'Notes on Irish legal history', *NILQ*, 7 (1947), 121.

is appreciative of those efforts, it is not uncritical. Within the pages that follow there will also be found an agenda of unfinished business. The agenda is a lengthy one.

1.2 CHRONOLOGICAL SURVEYS

Published surveys concentrating on specific historical periods have varied considerably both in the approach adopted towards legal history and in the depth of treatment extended. A convenient point of departure is S.G. Ellis, *Tudor Ireland: crown, community and the conflict of cultures, 1470–1603* (London and New York, 1985), and especially chapter 6. Ellis' principal object is to examine the actual historical record afresh in order to establish the extent to which it could be claimed that a Tudor-style revolution in government had occurred equally in Ireland. It is now accepted that major developments did indeed take place in England under the Tudors – the rise of parliament, the emergence of additional courts of law, the inauguration of a host of other institutional changes, even the birth of a novel species of law report. In Ireland, however, as Ellis demonstrates, a gap was to open up between the plans mooted by the Dublin government, plans usually based on English precedent, and that government's actually concluded achievements, and this became a distinctive feature in the legal system no less than in the system of financial administration. As for the individual achievements themselves it additionally needs to be understood, Ellis argues, that these were too frequently calculated to fail to win endorsement from two quarters where endorsement mattered: Gaelic society was alienated by the disintegration of the gradualist reform policy of 'surrender and regrant' and the Old English, with a long history of representation in the Irish parliament, grew increasingly suspicious of the government's programme. None of this augured well for the future. Much of what Ellis writes in chapter 6 always to the point, on such matters as the condition and procedures of the common law courts, the growth of conciliar jurisdiction and the role of the shrievalty, is a condensed version of much fuller discussion exhibited in his complementary volume, *Reform and revival: English government in Ireland, 1470–1534* (Woodbridge, Suffolk and New York, 1986).

Questions of acculturation and assimilation substantially dominate the history of Ireland in the period before 1600. So far as the legal system is concerned, the task is to measure the influence of common law and Gaelic or brehon law each upon the other. G. MacNiocaill and K. Nicholls have latterly made important contributions in this area. MacNiocaill's 'The interaction of laws' in J. Lydon (ed.), *The English in medieval Ireland* (Dublin, 1984), p. 105, provides an up-to-date report fashioned on the salient, if sometimes difficult, evidence. The chapter on law in Nicholls' pioneering work, *Gaelic and gaelicized Ireland in the middle ages* (Dublin, 1972), presents a complementary viewpoint. Two collections of documents edited by Nicholls also repay scrutiny for the light they cast on the interpenetration of legal ideas during this transitional phase: 'Some documents on Irish law and custom in the sixteenth century', *Anal Hib*, 26 (1970), 103 and **The O Doyne (Ó Duinn) manuscript* (Dublin, IMC, 1983).

In an important book, *Sir John Davies and the conquest of Ireland: a study in legal imperialism* (Cambridge, 1985), H.S. Pawlisch resumes the story of Irish law at the conclusion of the Nine Years War (1594–1603). As a law officer of the crown, Davies played a major role in consolidating the Elizabethan conquest of the island and an evaluation of his role was patently overdue. Pawlisch builds his study around a selection of the important test cases which Davies included in his law reports, Ireland's first, published in Dublin in 1615. Supplying many missing details from the manuscript sources, Pawlisch endeavours to explain the underlying significance of these cases in terms of the Dublin government's relationship with Gaelic Ireland and with the Old English. Special stress is laid on the use made, in accordance with the apparent constitutional practice of Jacobean Ireland, of resolutions of the judges sitting in conclave as a source of law. Pawlisch analyses six of the eleven cases in Davies' reports – gavelkind, tanistry, the royal fishery of the Bann, mandates, customs payable for merchandise and mixed monies. Proxies, a seventh, is the subject of separate scrutiny by him subsequently: 'Sir John Davies' law reports and the case of proxies', *IJ*, 17 (1982), 368. Regrettably, Pawlisch barely hints at Davies' importance to later generations of historically-minded Irish lawyers. This is certainly an aspect of Davies' achievement that calls for further investigation.

Davies was equally celebrated as one of the principal architects of the Plantation of Ulster. The Plantation was preceded by the flight of the earls, O'Neill and O'Donnell, in 1607, and by the rebellion of O'Doherty in 1608. Various legal questions had then to be attended to before the Plantation proper could begin. These preliminaries are studied in a trio of papers by F.W. Harris: 'Matters relating to the indictments of "the fugitive earls and their principal adherents"', *IJ*, 18 (1983), 344; 'The rebellion of Sir Cahir O'Doherty and its legal aftermath', *IJ*, 15 (1980), 298; 'The commission of 1609: legal aspects', *Stud Hib*, 20 (1980), 31.

In 1622 royal commissioners recommended the adoption of a package of legal and judicial reforms. These have now been reprinted, accompanied by an introduction and commentary: G.J. Hand and V.W. Treadwell, 'His majesty's directions for ordering and settling the courts within his kingdom of Ireland, 1622', *Anal Hib*, 26 (1970), 177. An omnium gatherum of miscellaneous reforms, the directions highlight many of the perceived defects in the Irish law of the period. Interestingly, only two out of the total of 47 directions were aimed at the common law courts, and this affords striking proof of the major contemporary importance of other jurisdictions – the council, chancery, the presidency courts and the ecclesiastical courts. Hand and Treadwell allude to the question of the impact of the 1622 directions on the legal practice of the time but do not discuss this in detail. Yet another task to be shouldered can thus be identified. A few suggestions as to how it might be approached may be advanced. First, as regards the short-term impact, promising leads are to be found in the surviving documentation apropos the protracted *Gifford v. Loftus* litigation which commenced in 1636,[5] and in the published exchanges on the law and the constitution which took place between the Irish judges and Patrick Darcy in 1641.[6] Secondly, in relation to the longer term, it would seem plain that by the early nineteenth century the directions had been relegated to oblivion. This is the likeliest explanation for the ignorance of the tenor of direction VII ('choyce of sheriffs') in the otherwise extraordinarily well-informed literature and debate of 1838 on the history of appointing Irish sheriffs.[7] Some caution is warranted nevertheless, for it is passing strange that, in apparent contrast, the parallel directions of 1622 'concerning the state of the church of Ireland' were sufficiently well-known the previous century to be referred to verbatim in an important dispute on impropriate tithes

---

5 HMC, *9th report* (1883), appendix, 293 ff (mss of marquis of Drogheda).
6 P. Darcy, *An argument delivered ... by the express order of the House of Commons* (Waterford, 1643).
7 A barrister (H.H. Joy?), *Letter to the rt hon Lord Lyndhurst, on the appointment of sheriffs in Ireland, under the earl of Mulgrave* (London and Dublin, 1838); *Hansard, 3rd series*, vol. 43, col 989, House of Lords, 25 June 1838.

which progressed on appeal from the Irish chancery to the House of Lords in the 1750s.[8]

Whilst recent studies devoted to the Old English and to the lord deputyship of Strafford (1635–41) necessarily touch on a number of legal and constitutional issues, the next detailed survey of the legal system is that furnished by T.C. Barnard in a chapter in his *Cromwellian Ireland* (Oxford, 1976). Barnard focuses attention on the momentous year of 1655 that saw both the re-establishment of the four courts and the equally suggestive revival of the commission of the peace. Thereafter, as the author points out, the prospect of more radical reforms did indeed recede. Modest changes nevertheless appear to have been pushed through, in the law of debt and in practice and procedure generally. Significantly, malpractices perpetrated by sheriffs were the object of continuing scrutiny. In Ireland as in England suspicion of the more extreme politicians stopped the law reform movement almost dead in its tracks.

There now ensues a very long break in the historical continuity, and, sadly, when accounts of the Irish legal system are again provided, the insights on offer are somewhat less satisfying – a reflection, perhaps, not only of the sparseness of recent original research but also of the immensity of the tasks of comprehension and interpretation for periods closer to the present day. M. Wall's pamphlet, *The penal laws, 1691–1760* (Dundalk, 1976), is a useful introduction to a difficult topic. However, she ignores several distinct aspects, a number of practical questions and the ultimate legacy bequeathed by this misshapen religious penal code to Irish law. The last point should not be underestimated. The reach of laws of persecution and discrimination is invariably insidious and far-flung: penal law elements are discernible in practical legal problems that surfaced in Ireland as recently as early this century.[9] A trained lawyer is definitely to be encouraged to travel the same ground as the late Mrs Wall and to be, if anything, even more adventurous.

There is a short impressionistic account of Irish law in chapter 2 of R.B. McDowell's *Ireland in the age of imperialism and revolution, 1760–1801* (Oxford, 1979). The courts of law are awarded a separate chapter in the same writer's *The Irish administration, 1801–1914* (London and Toronto, 1964) which thus in effect continues the story. Whilst the

---

8 *Hawtrey v. Daniel* (1760) 7 Bro 21, 3 Eng Rep 14.
9 *Swifte v. Attorney-General* [1910] 2 IR 140; [1912] AC 276.

latter arrangement is more satisfactory and McDowell's familiarity with the official sources, especially the parliamentary papers, makes him as ever a more than reliable guide, he somehow fails to convey the full flavour of the immensity of the changes wrought in the nineteenth century. 'Legal developments, 1801–79', a chapter contributed by J.C. Brady to volume v of *A new history of Ireland* (Oxford, 1989), at p. 451, concentrates rather less on the institutional and achieves greater balance. Brady places the majority of the nineteenth-century changes firmly within a constitutional setting where the fact of the union with Great Britain ensured that ultimately Ireland would share in the benefits of progressive legislation. A succession of reformist laws ensued as, one by one, the abuses that had so often previously attracted the attention of some parliamentary inquiry or another were finally set right. Simplified procedure, easier conveyancing, a fusion of law and equity, reforms in property law – these were to be the highlights.

W.N. Osborough, 'Law in Ireland 1916–1926', *NILQ*, 23 (1972), 48, attempts a bird's-eye view of the legal system in a critical decade of the modern era which witnessed, in rapid succession, rebellion, partition (involving secession for Northern Ireland) and independence (for the territory which is now the Republic of Ireland). The same author has also sought to portray the ineluctable disappearance of the old order against the surely symbolic background of insurance litigation in his 'Forcibly commandeered transport and owner's insurance: the deciding of two test cases in the 1920s', *IJ*, 11 (1976), 105. Within this revolutionary period Dáil Eireann established its own court system in opposition to the traditional system that continued to operate under British auspices. The unusual story of this rival court system has now been comprehensively covered: C. Davitt (the late Mr Justice Davitt), 'Civil jurisdiction of the courts of the Irish republic, 1920–1922', *IJ*, 3 (1968), 112; J.P. Casey, 'Republican courts in Ireland, 1919–1922', *IJ*, 5 (1970), 321 and 'The genesis of the Dáil courts', *IJ*, 9 (1974), 326.

1.3 CONSTITUTIONAL HISTORY

Prima facie, constitutional history appears to be the branch of Irish legal history best served by recent writers. In this it may owe something to the close connection with political history and to more readily discernible lines of inquiry. To begin with, latter years have seen the publication of significant monographs on a host of themes never far from the preoccupations of the constitutional historian. Examples are, listing the items in an historical chronology: B. Bradshaw, *The Irish constitutional revolution of the sixteenth century* (Cambridge, 1979); J.G. Simms, *Jacobite Ireland, 1685–91* (London, 1969); E.M. Johnston, *Great Britain and Ireland, 1760–1800: a study in political administration* (Edinburgh and London, 1963); R.B. McDowell, *Ireland in the age of imperialism and revolution, 1760–1801*; B. Inglis, *The freedom of the press in Ireland, 1784–1841* (London, 1954); G.C. Bolton, *The passing of the Irish act of union* (London, 1966); R.B. McDowell, *The Irish convention, 1917–1918* (London, 1970); J. McColgan, *British policy and the Irish administration, 1920–22* (London, 1983).

Parliamentary history (that of the pre-union Irish parliament) has earned considerable attention. There are two useful collections of essays: B. Farrell (ed.), *The Irish parliamentary tradition* (Dublin and New York, 1973) and A. Cosgrove and J.I. McGuire (eds), *Parliament and community: Historical Studies XIV* (Belfast, 1983). In addition, the study of individual parliaments – a genre popularized by C.L. Falkiner[10] – continues to attract historians, and the resulting reports have appeared at intervals in the various learned journals. Surveys concentrating on parliamentary affairs in the years 1692 and 1753 will also be found in: T. Bartlett and D.W. Hayton (eds), *Penal era and golden age: essays in Irish history, 1690–1800* (Belfast, 1979). Accounts of the background to specific legislation have also begun to emerge. Examples are two surveys put together by J.G. Simms: 'The bishops' banishment act of 1697', *IHS*, 17 (1970–1), 185; and 'The making of a penal law, 1703–4', *IHS*, 12 (1960–1), 105. A proportion of this variegated writing alludes only fleetingly to mainstream constitutional history, but no serious student of the subject can afford to overlook any of it.

A few articles dealing with more technical questions for the pre-union period deserve separate listing. A. Clarke has continued, where others had left off,[11] a chronological narrative of the legislative restrictions on the competence of the Irish parliament: 'The history of Poynings' Law, 1615–1641', *IHS*, 18 (1972–3), 207. Clarke has also surveyed the constitutional grievances of the political opposition of 1640–1: 'The policies of the "Old English" in parliament, 1640–41',

---

10 'The parliament of Ireland under the Tudor sovereigns', *PRIA*, 25 (1904–5), section C, 508.
11 R.D. Edwards and T.W. Moody, 'The history of Poynings' Law: part I', *IHS*, 2 (1940–1), 241.

in: J.L. McCracken (ed.), *Historical Studies V* (London, 1965), p. 85. William Molyneux's seminal tract of 1698, *The case of Ireland's being bound by acts of parliament of England stated*, has been re-assessed from a novel perspective by P. Kelly: 'The Irish woollen export prohibition act of 1699: Kearney revisited', *IESH*, 7 (1980), 22; and the same author has concerned himself with matters of textual analysis: 'The printer's copy of the ms. of Molyneux's *The case of Ireland's being bound ...* (1698)', *Long Room* (Bulletin of the Friends of the Library, Trinity College, Dublin), 18–19 (1979), 7. An important offering from G.J. Hand, 'The Irish military establishment from the restoration to the union', *IJ*, 3 (1968), 330, breaks more fresh ground.[12] J.C. Beckett's 'Anglo-Irish constitutional relations in the later eighteenth century', *IHS*, 14 (1964–5), 21 is an excellent introduction to the vexed question of how the constitution worked in practice between 1782 and 1800, the era of Grattan's parliament.

The political turmoil in the country early in the present century again brought constitutional issues to the forefront of Irish life. The continuing influence on contemporary Irish society of the manner of their resolution at that time has ensured a steady flow of associated monographs and papers. An embarrassment of material entails that it is not always simple to identify contributions to mainstream constitutional history. McDowell's study of the abortive Irish convention of 1918, referred to earlier, plainly qualifies, as do two complementary papers on the Government of Ireland Act 1920: D.G. Boyce, 'British conservative opinion, the Ulster question and the partition of Ireland, 1919–21', *IHS*, 17 (1970), 85; N. Mansergh, 'The Government of Ireland Act 1920: its origins and purpose', in: J. Barry (ed.), *Historical Studies IX* (Belfast, 1974). The partition of Ireland was inaugurated under the terms of the act of 1920. Its later consolidation is attributable to the collapse of the inter-governmental boundary commission appointed in accordance with article 12 of the Anglo-Irish treaty of 1921. The commission's proposed award and the report upon which it was based were both suppressed in 1925. That report has now been published, together with a helpful introduction: G.J. Hand (ed.), *The report of the Irish boundary commission 1925* (Shannon, 1969). The events in Ireland in the early 1920s left many legal and constitutional conundrums unresolved. One of these, the fate of the Irish repre-

---

12 Professor Hand's views were taken into account in modern litigation: *In re Royal Hospital Kilmainham* [1966] IR 451.

sentative peers, is engagingly scrutinized in: C.E. Lysaght, 'The Irish peers and the House of Lords', *NILQ*, 18 (1967), 277.

A selection of issues in the modern constitutional history of the South have already been the subject of scholarly appraisal. In a four-part series B. Farrell has traced 'The drafting of the Irish Free State constitution', *IJ*, 5 (1970), 115, 343; 6 (1971), 111, 345. Farrell's work is supplemented by T. Towey, 'Hugh Kennedy and the constitutional development of the Irish Free State, 1922–23', *IJ*, 12 (1977), 355. D. McMahon has considered the curious interlude when Mr de Valera sought to translate Kennedy, then the chief justice, to the vacant governor-generalship: 'The chief justice and the governor-general controversy in 1932', *IJ*, 17 (1982), 145; and M. Gallagher the controversial circumstances surrounding the resignation of President Ó Dálaigh in 1976: 'The presidency of the republic of Ireland: implications of the "Donegan" affair', *Parliamentary Affairs*, 30 (1977), 373. J.P. Casey's exhaustive monograph, *The office of the attorney general in Ireland* (Dublin, 1980), has a good deal to say on various aspects of recent constitutional history as well as on more mundane matters of criminal procedure, work with which the office of the attorney general was long historically connected.

In the case of the modern constitutional history of Northern Ireland there is again much new writing. Two particular studies may nonetheless be singled out: the late E. Graham's 'Religion and education: the constitutional problem', *NILQ*, 33 (1982), 20 and D. Harkness' 'The difficulties of devolution: the post-war debate at Stormont', *IJ*, 13 (1977), 176.[13] Since the present period of serious unrest started in Northern Ireland in 1968 there has of course been no dearth of further constitutional experimentation. Issues of law and order have been equally to the fore. In retrospect, the collapse of a combined law and order pact of an earlier year, 1922, was not a good omen. A contemporary report on the collapse of this particular pact has also now been edited: K. Boyle, 'The Tallents report on the Craig-Collins pact of 30 March 1922', *IJ*, 12 (1977), 151.

The comparative flood of writing in the field of Irish constitutional history cannot unfortunately conceal the fact that a host of problems here too still lies unexamined. A short inventory would include: the position of the church establishment prior to 1869, the use of the act

---

13 Mr Graham, a young scholar of great promise, was murdered by terrorist gunmen in 1983 outside the law faculty at Queen's University, Belfast.

of state as a source of law in the seventeenth century, the consequences of the non-enactment of a bill of rights in the wake of the revolution of 1688, the progress of Catholic emancipation and the rise of habeas corpus. Nor has anything like the last word been said on the nature of the constitutional relationship linking Ireland and Britain both before and after the act of union. On this the historian must be prepared to cast his net very wide indeed: the jurisdictional complexity of ecclesiastical and admiralty appeals, the extraordinary episode of the transportation convoy returned from Newfoundland in 1781,[14] and the legally inspired obstruction of the exertions of the press-gang in 1805 (see A. Hamilton, 'A treatise on impressing', *IJ*, 8 (1973), edited and with an introduction by W.N. Osborough), for example, would all deserve to be taken into consideration.

A major lacuna in the writing to date has been the almost total failure to utilize the evidence contained in the law reports. Cases such as *Parliament in Ireland* (1613),[15] *Neale v. Cottingham* (1770),[16] *Knox v. Gavan* (1836),[17] *Ex parte Selwyn* (1872),[18] *O'Keeffe v. Cullen* (1873)[19] and *Hunter v. Coleman* (1914)[20] all have important ramifications, and moreover point to fresh directions in research. But of the heritage of Irish constitutional case-law, only *Wright v. Fitzgerald* (1798),[21] *Egan v. Macready* (1921)[22] and one or two others on police powers figure among the few that have captured any kind of interest: P. O'Higgins, '*Wright v. Fitzgerald* revisited', *Modern Law Review*, 25 (1962), 413 and R.F.V. Heuston, *Essays in constitutional law* (London, 1961). An exception may also be claimed in respect of P.S.J. Langan, 'Irish material from the state trials', *NILQ*, 18 (1967), 428; 19 (1968), 48, 189, 299.

1.4 THE COURTS OF LAW

No extended survey has been attempted for any of the common law courts of king's bench, common pleas and exchequer prior to their union under the judicature reforms of 1877. The destruction of public records that occurred at the Four Courts in Dublin in 1922 naturally has hardly encouraged any scholar to embark upon the enterprise.

14 HMC, *13th rep, appendix*, vol. 1 (1892), 539ff (Fortescue mss).
15 12 Co Rep 110, 77 Eng Rep 1386.   16 Wallis by Lyne 54.
17 1 Jones 190.   18 36 JP 54.   19 IR 7 CL 319.
20 [1914] 2 IR 372.   21 27 How. St. Tr. 759.   22 [1921] 1 IR 265.

Those anxious to glean something of the modern history of these courts must accordingly rely principally on the sketch given in Newark's 'Notes', as amplified by Wood's *Guide* and R.B. McDowell's summary for the nineteenth century. In respect of two earlier periods, the Tudor and Cromwellian, the recent books by Ellis and Barnard help to round out the picture. In addition, the determined sleuth will uncover many incidental references to the courts, particularly to king's bench, in the printed sources and in published articles. Of the three courts, exchequer is an obvious first choice for meticulous examination. The surviving records, if not abundant, are at least ample; an added incentive is the possession by the court (c.1600–1850) of a substantial equity jurisdiction. The court of chancery, rather longer in the business of attending to equity matters (in addition to much else besides), no less craves for attention. Here however a start has been made. Sets of chancery pleadings were salvaged from the Four Courts fire of 1922 and some of these have already been printed: their value as an historical source is increasingly acknowledged by scholars. In addition, an edition has been published of seventeenth-century rules of practice: G.J. Hand, 'Rules and orders to be observed in the proceedings of causes in the high court of chancery in Ireland, 1659', *IJ*, 9 (1974), 110.

Appeals from the Irish courts could find their way to the English king's bench and House of Lords and in the eighteenth century the practice was instituted of insisting on a printed form of appeal. Extant collections of these printed appeals constitute a source of additional information on all kinds of issues. L. Redmond, 'Irish appeals to the House of Lords in the eighteenth century', *Anal Hib*, 23 (1966), 245, is a handy guide.

Under the Tudors and Stuarts the work of the common law courts was not only complemented but also to an extent even superseded, as in England, by the activities of conciliar and prerogative courts. Substantial progress has latterly been made in the endeavour to fix both the rationale and the precise sphere of operations of several of these tribunals. Two studies on the Irish court of wards (H.F. Kearney, 'The court of wards and liveries in Ireland, 1622–1641', *PRIA*, 57 (1954–6), section C, 29; V. Treadwell, 'The Irish court of wards under James I', *IHS*, 12 (1960–1), 1) naturally focus on administrative questions, and much light is cast on late feudal practice in Ireland with regard to wardship. J.G. Crawford has tackled the Irish equivalent of star chamber: 'The origins of the court of castle chamber: a star chamber jurisdiction in Ireland', *AJLH*, 24 (1980), 72. Crawford re-examines the views of Wood, propounded by the latter in a much earlier account,[23] particularly as regards the motive behind the formal establishment of the court in 1571, a decision that came after many false starts reaching back as far as the ordinances of 1534.[24] The relationship between castle chamber and the judicial business transacted before the full council awaits further investigation.

Presidency courts, set up under like prerogative authority, lasted in Ireland from 1569 to 1672. Three such courts had originally been envisaged, one for each of the provinces other than Leinster. That for Ulster was never proceeded with, little is known of the Connacht court and L. Irwin's pioneering survey ('The Irish presidency courts, 1569–1672', *IJ*, 12 (1977), 106) is centred around the better-documented Munster court. More will be found on the latter court in Barnard's reconstruction of its activities during the interregnum: *Cromwellian Ireland*, p. 262. The long-term impact of the presidency courts on the Irish legal system deserves close scrutiny. It seems certain, however, that it was from this source that the Irish courts of equity derived their jurisdiction to 'quiet possession', a jurisdiction not infrequently called in aid until the late nineteenth century.[25]

The ecclesiastical courts, linked formally with the Church of Ireland prior to the latter's disestablishment in 1869, have been almost universally neglected, with the result, apart from Wood's *Guide*, it is extremely difficult to gather even the most elementary of details regarding such curiosities as the courts of delegates and of the prerogative and faculties and the Irish counterpart of the high commission. A modicum of extraneous detail is available in discussions of tithe law, an understandable preoccupation of the historian of Irish agrarian unrest. A more detailed treatment of this branch of law is forthcoming from M. Bric in a recent paper: *PRIA*, 80 (1986), section C, p. 271. There is a clear need to awaken interest in this area of Irish legal history: an edition of the king's directions of 1622, a set paralleling those for the courts, and a reprinting of the Church of Ireland canons of 1634 would be helpful.

23 H. Wood, 'The court of castle chamber or star chamber of Ireland', *PRIA*, 32 (1913–16), section C, 152.
24 State Papers, Henry VIII, vol. 2, 207.
25 See the judgment of Lord Lifford L.C. in *Stewart v. Stewart* (1770) Wallis by Lyne 97 and that of Mr Justice Robinson in *The King v. Reily* (1784), reported at Ir Term Rep 204.

Admiralty jurisdiction has fared much better. Two happily complementary studies (J.C. Appleby and M. O'Dowd, 'The Irish admiralty: its organisation and development, c.1570–1640', *IHS*, 24 (1985), 229; D.E.C. Yale, 'Notes on the jurisdiction of the admiralty in Ireland', *IJ*, 3 (1968), 146) trace the growth of the jurisdiction from the point in the 1570s when an Irish court was first established down to the reconstruction of the court in 1867. Appleby and O'Dowd reveal how at the outset the Dublin court was thwarted in the attempt to consolidate its authority by the joint opposition of the lord deputy and council and by the corporate towns, all of whom claimed likewise to be in a position to attend to admiralty matters. An early dispute between court and council turned on the contentious issue of claims arising from the loss of vessels that formed part of the Spanish Armada of 1588 – an episode still capable of raising intriguing legal problems.[26] Both studies emphasize the implications of the consistent refusal by the high court of admiralty in London to permit the courts in Ireland to exercise an original jurisdiction in prize. This state of affairs prevailed even after the extinction of the various vice-admiralty courts and the enactment of regulatory legislation by Grattan's parliament.

Other courts are best considered together. The palatinate of Ormonde, co-terminous with an area roughly corresponding to that of the modern county Tipperary, was established in the early fourteenth century and survived various vicissitudes[27] until it was finally abolished on the attainder of the second duke of Ormonde in 1715, who fell with Bolingbroke in the Jacobite conspiracy. V.T.H. Delany has provided an account of the legal system of this most celebrated of the Irish palatinates, though by no means exhausting the available source material: 'The palatinate court of the liberty of Tipperary', *AJLH*, 5 (1961), 95. In the 1920s and 1930s the Irish manor courts evinced some attention when records from two Dublin manors, those of Crumlin and Esker, and from the manor of Dunluce in Antrim were introduced to the public.[28] The same level of interest has hardly been maintained. C.A. Empey, however, has made extensive use of materials relating to

---

26 Note, 'Discoveries from Armada wrecks', *IJ*, 5 (1970), 88.
27 Including the resumption of the palatinate by the crown in the time of James I: see E.S. Bade, 'A princely judgment (the earl of Ormond's case)', *Minnesota Law Review*, 23 (1934), 925.
28 E. Curtis, 'The courtbook of Esker and Crumlin, 1592–1600', *JRSAI*, 59 (1929), 45, 128; 60 (1930), 38, 137; J.B. Hamilton (ed.), *Records of the court leet, manor of Dunluce, Co. Antrim, held in Ballymoney* (Ballymoney, 1934).

another manor court ('Medieval Knocktopher: a study in manorial settlement – II', *Old Kilkenny Review*, 2 (1983), 441) and T.G.F. Paterson has described the contents of a further collection of manor court rolls belonging to the 1620s: 'The Armagh manor court rolls', *Seanchas Ardmhacha*, 2 (1957), 295. Borough courts too have nearly been lost sight of. Records of the Dublin court of conscience which remained active until 1924 do survive, however, and J.L.J. Hughes has sketched a portrait of that court in his 'The Dublin court of conscience', *Dublin Historical Record*, 15 (1958–9), 42. Unfortunately, Hughes omitted to comb the law reports for further information on the court, a strategy that would have paid handsome dividends.[29] The magistrates' courts were manned principally by the unpaid justices of the peace, holders of an office which made a relatively late appearance in Ireland for reasons explained by R. Frame, 'The medieval Irish keepers of the peace', *IJ*, 2 (1967), 308. A brief overview of the history for the office subsequent to 1800 will be found in: W.N. Osborough's introduction to E.A. Comerton, *A handbook of the Magistrates' Courts Act (N.I.) 1964* (Belfast, 1968), p. xxxvii. O. MacDonagh has resurrected one curious episode in which an *ex officio* J.P. from Cork was the principal protagonist: 'The last bill of pains and penalties: the case of Daniel O'Sullivan 1869', *IHS*, 19 (1974–5), 136.

1.5 SUBSTANTIVE LAW

Particular branches of Irish substantive law have attracted a modest amount of attention, though detailed scrutiny is still a rarity. Land law, perhaps inevitably, has been a major focus of interest. Among a wealth of relevant material, two discussions of quite different facets to Irish property law may be singled out, J.G. Simms' *The Williamite confiscation in Ireland, 1690–1703* (London, 1956) and J.C. Brady's 'Legal developments to 1879', a chapter contributed to the volume on the nineteenth century in *A new history of Ireland*. Brady conducts the reader through the intricacies of both procedural and substantive reforms, all of immense importance in terms of the landlord-tenant relationship, with considerable dexterity. The same author's *Religion and the law of charities in Ireland* (Belfast, n.d. (1966)) is a skilled introduction to both charities law itself and historical aspects of

---

29 See *Maguire v. James* (1824) Batty & Smith 100; *Cairnes v. Whelan* (1828) 1 Hudson & Brooke 552; *Carroll v. Harty* (1832) Glascock 220; *Coghlan v. Boland* (1838) 1 ILR 63.

charities administration. On the controversial charities legislation of 1844, D.A. Kerr's account in his *Peel, priests and politics* (Oxford, 1982) should not be missed.

Family law has started belatedly to intrigue the historian. Two papers in a collection edited by A. Cosgrove, *Marriage in Ireland* (Dublin, 1985), are particularly to be recommended, that by Cosgrove himself, 'Marriage in medieval Ireland', a survey which trespasses into the modern period (at p. 25), and that by P.J. Corish, 'Catholic marriage under the penal code' (at p. 67). Additional information of considerable fascination is supplied in K. Simms, 'The legal position of Irishwomen in the later middle ages', *IJ*, 10 (1975), 97. The historical dimension to labour law has been less well catered for, though much pertinent detail can be tracked down in two specialist journals, *Saothar* (Journal of the Irish Labour History Society) and *Irish Economic and Social History*. Mention may be made of P. Park's exploratory foray, 'The combination acts in Ireland, 1727–1825', *IJ*, 14 (1979), 340. W.N. Osborough's 'Irish law and the rights of the national schoolteacher', *IJ*, 14 (1979), 36, 304 covers the historical context.

The Irish malicious injuries code has been an unique system of imposing liability upon local authorities in respect primarily of damage to property. Its historical antecedents are the subject of careful examination in the introductory chapter of a new text-book: D.S. Greer and V.A. Mitchell, *Compensation for criminal damage to property* (Belfast, 1982).

Two reports by the Irish Law Reform Commission (*Vagrancy and related offences* (Dublin, 1985); *Offences against the Dublin police acts and related offences* (Dublin, 1985)) contain sections on the historical evolution of the present regime of minor offences known to Irish law. As regards more serious offences, the only major synopsis is P. O'Higgins, 'Blasphemy in Irish law', *Modern Law Review*, 23 (1960), 151. Two topics in nineteenth-century criminal procedure have not been ignored however, both of them connected with the system of trial by jury – jury-packing (J.F. McEldowney, 'The case of *The Queen v. McKenna* (1869) and jury packing in Ireland', *IJ*, 12 (1977), 339) and peremptory challenges in prosecutions for non-capital felonies (D.S. Johnson, 'The trials of Sam Gray', *IJ*, 20 (1985), 109). These two papers add more than a dash of colour to the study of the management of criminal prosecutions in the Ireland of the time. Many other questions merit equally detailed treatment – jurisdictional competence, the dock brief and the work of the Irish equivalent of the court for crown cases reserved, for instance.

1.6 PUBLIC ADMINISTRATION

Facets of the history of public administration are of absorbing interest to the legal historian. In the case of Ireland, R.B. McDowell's *The Irish administration, 1801–1914* is now the standard guide. Excellent studies have also been published on the history of the provision of facilities (such as they were) for deserted and orphan children (J. Robins, *The lost children: a study of charity children in Ireland, 1700–1900* (Dublin, 1980)) and for the mentally ill (M. Finnane, *Insanity and the insane in post-famine Ireland* (London, 1981)). Altogether different is the account of the legal background to canal development in Ireland to be found in the opening chapter of V.T.H. and D.R. Delany, *The canals of the south of Ireland* (Newton Abbot, 1966).

O. MacDonagh's *The inspector general: Sir Jeremiah Fitzpatrick and the politics of social reform, 1783–1802* (London, 1981) dwells on the late eighteenth-century phenomenon of Irish penal reform. A series of articles on prison questions enables track to be maintained of one particular topic of continuing social concern: A.J. Nowlan, 'Kilmainham jail', *Dublin Historical Record*, 15 (1960), 105; H. Heaney, 'Ireland's penitentiary, 1820–1831; an experiment that failed', *Stud Hib*, 14 (1974), 28; R.S.E. Hinde, 'Sir Walter Crofton and the reform of the Irish convict system', *IJ*, 12 (1977), 115, 295; B.A. Smith, 'The Irish general prisons board, 1877–1885: efficient deterrence or bureaucratic ineptitude?', *IJ*, 15 (1980), 122; B.A. Smith, 'The Irish prison system, 1885–1914: land war to world war', *IJ*, 16 (1981), 316. W.N. Osborough's *Borstal in Ireland: custodial provision for the young adult offender, 1906–1974* (Dublin, 1975) brings aspects of the administrative record up to date. The same writer has furnished 'An outline history of the penal system in Ireland', published as an appendix to the *Report of the Committee of Inquiry into the Penal System*, Pl 3391 (Dublin, 1985), 181.

The history of policing has also provoked some original research. G. Broeker, *Rural disorder and police reform in Ireland, 1812–36* (London, 1970), examines policing in a singularly critical period. A three-part series by K. Boyle covers 'Police in Ireland before the union', *IJ*, 7

(1972) 115, 8 (1973), 90, 323. N.M. Dawson, 'Illicit distillation and the revenue police in Ireland in the eighteenth and nineteenth centuries', *IJ*, 12 (1977), 282 is self-explanatory. There are in addition many references to police questions in the general historiography of Ireland between 1800 and 1922. Three items may be highlighted: on policing against a background of agrarian unrest, L.P. Curtis Jr, *Coercion and conciliation* (Princeton, NJ, 1963), and on policing against one of subversion and revolution, R. Hawkins, 'Government versus secret societies: the Parnell era' in T.D. Williams (ed.), *Secret societies in Ireland* (Dublin and New York, 1973), p. 100 and the same author's 'Dublin castle and the Royal Irish Constabulary (1916–22)', in T.D. Williams (ed.), *The Irish struggle, 1916–26* (London, 1966), p. 100.

1.7 BIOGRAPHY

Obvious strides have been made in the writing of Irish legal biography. Two full-length lives have been published: V.T.H. Delany, *Christopher Palles (1831–1920)* (Dublin, 1960) and G.M. Golding, *George Gavan Duffy, 1882–1951* (Dublin, 1982). Pawlisch's book on *Sir John Davies and the conquest of Ireland* brings together an amount of data on its central figure (1569–1626). Barnard's *Cromwellian Ireland* includes cameos of each of the lawyers nominated for judicial appointment on the revival of the four courts in 1655. There is a separate account of the Irish career of the regicide John Cook (?1609–60) who went on to serve a stint as a judge of the Munster presidency court and who refused, on grounds of principle, to accept nomination in 1655 (p. 262).[30] The studies of the Irish admiralty from Appleby and O'Dowd and from Yale yield a good deal of fresh information on judges who held office in the admiralty court.

Separate profiles exist for a small number of others: Arthur Browne (1756–1805), civilian (P. O'Higgins, *NILQ*, 20 (1969), 255); William Sampson (1764–1836), emigrant lawyer (O'Higgins, *Dublin University Law Review*, 2 (1971), 45); William Ridgeway (1765–1817), law reporter (O'Higgins, *NILQ*, 18 (1967), 208); Thomas O'Hagan (1812–85), judge (J.F. McEldowney, *IJ*, 14 (1979), 360); James Shaw Willes (1814–72), judge (R.F.V. Heuston, *NILQ*, 16 (1965), 193); Hugh

---

30 Cook's reasons for declining appointment to the Dublin courts in 1655, contained in Bodl Rawlinson MS A 189, are printed as an appendix to E. MacLysaght, *Irish life in the seventeenth century* (Cork, 1939).

McCalmont Cairns (1819–82), judge (Heuston, *NILQ*, 26 (1975), 269); John Blake Powell (1861–1923), judge (J.F. Larkin, *IJ*, 20 (1985), 403); and Leo Kohn (1894–1961), constitutional author (G.J. Hand, 'A reconsideration of a German study of the Irish constitution of 1922', in Bieber, Blackman and Capotorti (eds), *Das Europa der zweiten Generation: Gedächtnisschrift für Christoph Sasse* (Kehl am Rhein – Strasburg, 1981). A number of Irish entries were originally included in the *Dictionary of national biography*. Revised and additional material will be found in: A.W. Simpson (ed.), *Biographical dictionary of the common law* (London, 1984) and in H. Boylan, *Dictionary of Irish biography* (Dublin, 1978).

The recent expenditure of effort on biographical writing serves to emphasize the kind of detailed and exhaustive research which is demanded and which has scarcely begun in earnest. The way forward will not be easy. Elementary biographical data on a large number of individuals is difficult to come by and an assessment of their precise contribution to Irish law will prove equally onerous.

1.8 THE PROFESSION, EDUCATION AND PUBLISHING

The history of the Irish legal profession has suffered from serious neglect. Some recent progress can, however, be reported. B. Bradshaw, *The dissolution of the religious orders in Ireland* (Cambridge, 1974), discusses the role of the Pale lawyers in the affairs of the Irish reformation parliaments of the 1530s. D.F. Cregan repeats a broadly similar exercise in respect of the politics of Jacobean Ireland ('Irish recusant lawyers in politics in the reign of James I', *IJ*, 5 (1970), 306) and has also examined 'Irish catholic admissions to the English inns of court, 1558–1625', *IJ*, 5 (1970), 95. E.M. Johnston, *Great Britain and Ireland, 1760–1800* (Edinburgh and London, 1963), has a section on the relationship of lawyers to politics in the last half of the eighteenth century (pp 235 ff). J.R. Hill investigates the same general question for the period immediately following catholic emancipation: 'The intelligentsia and Irish nationalism: the 1840s', *Stud Hib*, 20 (1980), 73. James Hardiman, in his appeal on behalf of Irish legal history made in 1843, had identified one group that he thought might appropriately take up the challenge: 'The time, talents, and learning of many of our young barristers might be ... usefully and ... profitably employed on works of this kind'.[31] Dr Hill's conclusions indicate one reason why Hardiman's confidence was doomed to disappointment: the young Irish lawyer of the period was commonly seduced by the lure of what he regarded as much more pressing business. D. Hogan's magisterial survey, *The legal profession in Ireland, 1789–1922* (Dublin, 1986), now covers much pertinent ground: hopefully, it may also serve as an inspiration to other practitioner-authors.

Among recently printed source material, special attention should be drawn to *M.R. O'Connell (ed.), *The correspondence of Daniel O'Connell*, 8 vols (Shannon (vols 1–3), Dublin (vols 4–8), IMC, 1972–80) and *E. Keane, P.B. Phair and T.U. Sadleir (eds), *King's Inns admission papers, 1607–1867* (Dublin, IMC, 1982). A descriptive account of the Black Book of King's Inns, the earliest record volume in the possession of the society and covering the years from 1607 to 1730, has now been provided by T. Power: *IJ*, 20 (1985), 135.

V.T.H. Delany has pioneered the examination of the history of Irish legal education: 'Legal studies in Trinity College Dublin since the foundation', *Hermathena*, 89 (1957), 3 and 'The history of legal education in Ireland', *Journal of Legal Education*, 12 (1960), 396. A few points of detail are added in a book review by Osborough: *IJ*, 18 (1983), 186.

The history of Irish legal publishing is also in its infancy. C.K. Boyle touches on the topic in a chapter on the Republic of Ireland in: W.L. Twining and J. Uglow (eds), *Law publishing and legal information: small jurisdictions of the British Isles* (London, 1981). Two detailed studies point the way forward, one published in 1943[32] and the other concentrating rather on the medieval period.[33] There is, in addition, a paper of exceptional interest from V.T.H. Delany which helps to illumine one dark corner, Irish law reporting: 'Lord Justice Christian and law reporting: a sidelight on Irish legal history', *NILQ*, 12 (1956–8), 46.

The subject is still at the stage where bibliographies and guides remain a necessity. P. O'Higgins has made major contributions to the field: *A bibliography of Irish trials and other legal proceedings* (Abingdon, 1986) and *A bibliography of periodical literature relating to Irish law*

---

31 *Tracts relating to Ireland*, II (1843), at p. 14.
32 D.B. Quinn, 'Government printing and the publication of the Irish statutes in the sixteenth century', *PRIA*, 49 (1943), section C, 45.
33 P. Brand, 'Ireland and the literature of the early common law', *IJ*, 16 (1981), 95.

(Belfast, 1966) with supplements in 1973 and 1983. The entries under the headings of 'legal history' and 'biography' in the latter publication, for example, will reveal the existence of many more articles than it has been possible to take note of here.

1.9 CONCLUSION

It should be evident from the preceding survey that major advances in Irish legal history have been registered in recent years from the point where the late F.H. Newark composed his 'Notes'. Yet equally, as has also been intimated, there remain vast gaps in our knowledge, many important tasks lie unperformed, and it may be surmized that the shade of James Hardiman accordingly has still not been sufficiently propitiated.

It is a valid exercise to seek to understand why this should be so. Plainly, the level of interest in, and the resultant commitment towards, this particular branch of Irish studies are both of crucial significance. Regrettably, each remains disturbingly low. Part of the explanation is to be found in a change in the pattern of litigation. Within the last thirty years only two cases brought before the courts on either side of the Irish border have necessitated prolonged investigation into problems of legal history: *Toome Eel Co. (N. Ireland) Ltd v. Cardwell* [1963] N.I. 92, [1966] N.I. 1; *In re Royal Hospital Kilmainham* [1966] IR 451. Litigation of an equivalent sort was much more plentiful in the past, a group of previous cases even prompting the formulation of fundamental questions over the implications for the law of such practically-oriented missions of historical inquiry: B. Murphy, 'The lawyer as historian: *Magna Carta* and the public right of fishery', *IJ*, 3 (1968), 131. The change in the pattern, a change attributable in part to the loss of a sense of organic evolution in Irish law, means that little practical encouragement is afforded the individual practitioner to foster an interest in matters of legal history. In the universities too the subject commands little more than marginal attention from among academic lawyers or professional historians.[34] They should not be too brusquely criticized for that. The lawyer discovers that it is hard enough to keep abreast of developments in modern law to be in a

---

34 Compare, for example, S.F.C. Milsom in his review of G.R. Elton, *F.W. Maitland*, in the *Times Literary Supplement*, 28 Feb. 1986.

position to spare the time to allow himself to be sidetracked by any kind of passion for the investigation of the past that he may have chanced to preserve. As for the historian, he, like the shareholder keeping an eye on his dividends, not unnaturally relishes a swift profit, and can be excused for failing to wish to acquire a novel form of expertise where mastering the recondite vocabulary of the sources is an obligatory and rather unappetising part of the course. An even weightier determinant perhaps is unique to Ireland: the impact of an isolationist cultural nationalism, analysed in this context by W.N. Osborough, 'Scholarship and the university law school', *DULJ*, 7 (1985), 1. A word by way of clarification is desirable. The legal history of Ireland for the modern period is substantially, if not exclusively, the history of English law in Ireland. In the Republic of Ireland today it may still be a difficult matter to arouse enthusiasm and money for the expenditure of time and effort on recapturing an indubitable portion of the cultural heritage which risks nonetheless being dismissed – by some, if not by the more discerning – as the unfortunate legacy of an alien imposition or, in the predictable accompanying rhetoric, 'a disaster best ignored'.[35]

---

35 I should like to thank Professor J.C. Brady, Mr M. Bric and Dr S.G. Ellis for their kindness in permitting me to consult material which was not yet published when this piece was written.

Recent writing on Irish legal history (2008)

2.1 INTRODUCTION

This survey of recent writing on Irish legal history is designed as a sequel to an earlier survey published in this journal in 1986. Two differences in approach merit notice. First, the survey is confined to legal history from the start of the modern era, which, for present purposes, is reckoned to date from the middle of the fifteenth century. Second, whereas the earlier survey was designed to cover all relevant published work up until 1985, the present essay (with a few exceptions) is restricted to published writings occurring since that date. The temptation to repair omissions in the earlier article has been resisted, partly because the sheer bulk of published work in the last twenty or so years left me with no other option. Vehicles for the publication of research in the area of Irish legal history have been proliferating in the last few decades. At one time there would have existed *Proceedings of the Royal Irish Academy*, the *Journal of the Royal Society of Antiquaries of Ireland*, *Irish Historical Studies* and the *Irish Jurist*. Now there are *Éire-Ireland* (started in 1966), *Irish Economic and Social History* (1974), *Saothar*, the journal of the Irish Labour History Society (1975), and *Eighteenth-Century Ireland* (1986). In addition, the year 1988 saw the establishment of a brand-new learned society immediately germane, the Irish Legal History Society, which has, to date, published some seventeen volumes, to all of which reference is made in the ensuing pages. Not to be ignored either in this brief inventory are the many new local history journals which from time to time do publish pertinent items on the law and its history on the island.

2.2 GENERAL NARRATIVES

Two chapters in Ellis' monograph on governance in Ireland under the first Tudor monarchs serve as a starting-point for the history of law in

Ireland in the modern era.[1] The first focuses on the fortunes of the common law, the second on the rise of Chancery as a court of law and the emergence of the Council as a key tribunal in the constitutional scheme of things. 'The evidence suggests', Ellis judiciously concludes,[2] 'that under the early Tudors the availability or otherwise of justice in the Pale [the area closest to, and including Dublin] was much as it was within the more settled shires of England and, less clearly, that the outlying counties were in no worse situation than the other borderlands of the Tudor state.'

One critical variation from the position in England was that, outside the Pale and down to the end of the Nine Years War in 1603, a totally different legal dispensation held sway: the brehon law of a Gaelic and gaelicized country. Earlier accounts[3] of the interaction of what were two distinct legal regimes – the common law and the brehon law – now perhaps require to be read in the light of new research by Patterson who furnishes fresh insight into the world of brehon law in the sixteenth century.[4] Evidence is thin, and not easy to interpret, but it does indeed look as if the final triumph of the common law in Ireland – reflected above all in the establishment of an all-Ireland pattern of assizes and assize circuits in the early seventeenth century[5] – was not so much of a surprise as might at first blush have been thought.

Pawlisch's monograph on Sir John Davies[6] effectively continues the narrative down to the 1620s, though the focus is narrow enough – the abandonment of gavelkind and tanistry (affecting the native community)[7]

1 S.G. Ellis, *Reform and revival: English government in Ireland, 1470–1534* (Royal Historical Society Studies in History 47) (Woodbridge, Suffolk and New York, 1986), chs. 4 and 5.
2 Ibid., p. 164.
3 E.g., G. MacNiocaill, 'The contact of Irish and common law', *NILQ*, 23 (1972), 16; idem, 'The interaction of laws' in J. Lydon (ed.), *The English in medieval Ireland* (Dublin, 1984), p. 105; *K. Nicholls, *The O'Doyne manuscript* (Dublin, 1984).
4 N. Patterson, 'Brehon law in late medieval Ireland: antiquarian and obsolete or traditional and functional?', *Cambridge Medieval Celtic Studies*, 17 (1989), 43; eadem, 'Gaelic law and the Tudor conquest of Ireland: the social background of the sixteenth-century recensions of the pseudo-historical Prologue to the Senchas már', *IHS*, 27 (1991), 193.
5 J. McCavitt, 'Good planets in their several spheares: the establishment of the assize circuits in early seventeenth-century Ireland', *IJ*, 24 (1989), 248.
6 H.S. Pawlisch, *Sir John Davies and the conquest of Ireland: a study in legal imperialism* (Cambridge, 1985).
7 Osborough deals separately with the eventual abolition in certain former Gaelic and gaelicized communities of the doctrine of tracts: 'The Irish custom of tracts', *IJ*, 32 (1997), 439, reprinted in W.N. Osborough, *Studies in Irish legal history* (Dublin, 1999), p. 64.

and the controversies over the 'mandates',[8] 'customs payable for merchandise' and 'mixed money' (affecting 'the colonial community'). The story of Irish law is taken up again in Hand and Treadwell's edition of James I's directions on legal and judicial reform for Ireland promulgated in 1622 following a report from royal commissioners.[9] The constitutional crisis of 1640–1, the subsequent rebellion and eventual formation of the Confederation of Kilkenny as a rival centre of governmental authority occupy the years prior to Oliver Cromwell's military campaigns and the institution of a republican form of government under the Lord Protector. Hitherto, no single legally oriented narrative has sought to capture the essence of the earlier of these momentous events.[10] With Cromwell and the Protectorate firmly in control, the situation, in historiographical terms, markedly improves with Barnard's classic account of the legal changes of the 1650s in his *Cromwellian Ireland*.[11]

Though insights into Irish law from the restoration of Charles II in 1660 down to the middle of the reign of George III are far from lacking, no all-embracing narrative accounts for this extended period have yet been furnished. Attempts to fill the vacuum after the 1780s will be found in Osborough's essay covering the years from 1796 to 1877[12] – with more detailed coverage of the meaning for Irish law of the rebellion of 1798 and its aftermath;[13] in Brady's chapter on the nineteenth century for *A new history of Ireland*;[14] and in a further contribution from Osborough addressing the years from 1916 to 1926.[15]

---

8   The mandates controversy in the early years of the reign of James I is also dealt with in detail in J. Crawford's, *A star chamber court in Ireland* (see below fn. 59).
9   *G.J. Hand and V.W. Treadwell, 'His majesty's directions for ordering and settling the courts within the kingdom of Ireland, 1622', *Anal Hib*, 26 (1970), 177.
10 Note should be taken, however, of M. Ó Siochrú, *Confederate Ireland, 1642–1649: a constitutional and political analysis* (Dublin, 1999).
11 T.C. Barnard, *Cromwellian Ireland: English government and reform in Ireland, 1649–1660* (London, 1975), ch 9.
12 'The Irish legal system, 1796–1877' in C. Costello (ed.), *The Four Courts: 200 years – essays to commemorate the bicentenary of the Four Courts* (Dublin, 1996), p. 33, reprinted in W.N. Osborough, *Studies* as in fn. 7, p. 239.
13 W.N. Osborough, 'Legal aspects of the 1798 rising, its suppression and the aftermath' in T. Bartlett, D. Dickson, D. Keogh and K. Whelan (eds), *1798: a bicentenary perspective* (Dublin, 2003), pp 437–68. See, too, P.C. Power, *The courts martial of 1798–9* (Carlow, 1997).
14 J.C. Brady, 'Legal developments, 1801–79' in W.E. Vaughan (ed.), *A new history of Ireland – v: Ireland under the Union: I* (Oxford, 1989), pp 451–81.
15 W.N. Osborough, 'Law in Ireland, 1916–1926', *NILQ*, 33 (1972), 48; reprinted in idem, *Studies* as in fn. 7, pp 270–95.

A monograph from Campbell examines the turmoil preceding and accompanying the establishment of the Irish Free State in 1922.[16] A sequel of sorts is supplied in Ó Longaigh, *Emergency law in independent Ireland, 1922–48*.[17]

2.3 CONSTITUTIONAL DEVELOPMENTS

Constitutional change in Ireland over the centuries continues to generate considerable interest. No less than four collections of essays have explored trends in political thought dating from the sixteenth century onwards, and these provide the context in which the various developments that occurred require to be placed.[18] Avowedly more legal studies remain comparatively rare, but here too some progress can be reported.

A major constitutional controversy in Ireland in the reign of Elizabeth I – that over the imposition of cess (in effect, a tax imposed by royal diktat) – is re-examined in Crawford's *Anglicizing the government of Ireland*.[19] A quarrel of a different stamp surfacing in the reign of Charles I that again concentrated on alleged abuses of executive power was the subject of Patrick Darcy's *An argument*, originally published in 1643.[20] *An argument* has been presented afresh in a helpful modern edition.[21] Associates of Lord Deputy Wentworth in the Irish government of the later 1630s – Lord Chancellor Bolton, Chief Justice Lowther, Bishop Bramhall and Sir George Radcliffe – who were attacked over these abuses, themselves figured in the abortive impeachment proceedings of 1641, now revisited by McCafferty.[22]

16 C. Campbell, *Emergency law in Ireland, 1918–1925* (Oxford, 1994). The same period is also dealt with in two books by Kotsonouris on the Dáil courts (see below fn. 74 and fn. 75).
17 S. Ó Longaigh, *Emergency law in independent Ireland, 1922–48* (Dublin, 2006).
18 D.G. Boyce, R. Eccleshall, V. Geoghegan (eds), *Political thought in Ireland since the seventeenth century* (London, 1993); H. Morgan (ed.), *Political ideology in Ireland, 1541–1641* (Dublin, 1999), J.H. Ohlmeyer (ed.), *Political thought in seventeenth-century Ireland* (Cambridge, 2000); S.J. Connolly (ed.), *Political ideas in eighteenth-century Ireland* (Dublin, 2000).
19 †J.G. Crawford, *Anglicizing the government of Ireland: the Irish privy council and the expansion of Tudor rule, 1556–1578* (Dublin, 1993), ch. 6.
20 P. Darcy, *An argument* (Waterford, 1643).
21 Patrick Darcy, *An argument*, edited by C.E.J. Caldicott (Camden Miscellany 31), *Camden 4th series*, 44 (London, 1992), 191.
22 J. McCafferty, 'To follow the late precedents of England: the Irish impeachment proceedings of 1641' in † D.S. Greer and N.M. Dawson (eds), *Mysteries and solutions in Irish legal history: Irish Legal History Society discourses and other papers, 1996–1999* (Dublin, 2001), p. 51.

For the eighteenth century Johnston-Liik's multi-volume *History of the Irish parliament* supplies an inexhaustible fount of knowledge.[23] McGrath's *The making of the eighteenth-century Irish constitution*[24] focuses on control of the revenue, but since constitutional progress here was intimately linked to the claim of the Irish House of Commons to the exercise of 'the sole right' to initiate financial legislation, more predictable constitutional fare is necessarily on offer.[25] Down to 1782 Poynings' Law of 1495 regulated the convening of parliaments and the passing of legislation. How in practice it had operated in the sixteenth and seventeenth centuries had previously been considered in a well-known group of articles in *Irish Historical Studies*.[26] The later history of the Law's operation – especially for the eighteenth century – is now the focus of separate studies from Kelly and Bergin,[27] and further findings from both these authors are awaited.

The deteriorating political situation as the eighteenth century nears its end is well captured in McDowell's *Ireland in the age of imperialism and revolution*,[28] one of several texts that sets out to chart and to explain the course of events leading up to, first, the 1798 rebellion and, second, the Act of Union of 1800.[29] Back in 1966 Bolton had treated of the

23 E.M. Johnston-Liik, *History of the Irish parliament 1692–1800: Commons, constituencies and statutes*, 6 vols (Belfast, 2002).
24 C.I. McGrath, *The making of the eighteenth-century Irish constitution: government, parliament and the revenue 1692–1714* (Dublin, 2000). See, too, his 'Central aspects of the eighteenth century constitutional framework in Ireland: the Government Supply Bill and Biennial Parliamentary Sessions 1715–82', *Eighteenth-Century Ireland*, 16 (2001), 9.
25 See ch. 3. The inferior status of the Irish parliament was prescribed by an Act of the British parliament in 1720, the background to which is examined in I. Victory, 'The making of the declaratory act of 1720' in G. O'Brien (ed.), *Parliament, politics, and people: essays in eighteenth-century Irish history* (Dublin, 1989), p. 14.
26 D.B. Quinn, 'The early interpretation of Poynings' Law 1494–1534', *IHS*, 2 (1940–1), 241; R.D. Edwards and T.W. Moody, 'The history of Poynings' Law: part 1, 1494–1615', *IHS*, 17 (1972–1973), 214.
27 J. Kelly, 'Monitoring the constitution: the operation of Poynings' Law in the 1760s' in D.W. Hayton (ed.), *The Irish parliament in the eighteenth century: the long apprenticeship* in *Parliamentary History*, 20: 1 (Edinburgh, 2001); 'The making of law in eighteenth-century Ireland: the significance and import of Poynings' Law' in †N.M. Dawson (ed.), *Reflections on law and history* (Dublin, 2006), p. 259; J. Bergin, 'Poynings' Law in the eighteenth century' in *Pages: Postgraduate Research in Progress*, Arts Faculty, UCD, Dublin, 1 (1994), 9–18.
28 R.B. McDowell, *Ireland in the age of imperialism and revolution, 1760–1801* (Oxford, 1979).
29 G. O'Brien, *Anglo-Irish politics in the age of Grattan and Pitt* (Dublin, 1987); T. Bartlett, *The fall and rise of the Irish nation: the Catholic question 1690–1830* (Dublin, 1992); J. Kelly, *Prelude to Union: Anglo-Irish politics in the 1780s* (Cork, 1992); D. Dickson, D. Keogh and K. Whelan (eds), *The United Irishmen* (Dublin, 1993). Other works dealing

enactment of this latter critical constitutional statute.[30] Geoghegan, in a new study, whilst recognising Bolton's 'towering achievement', has rescrutinized the reasons given for adoption of the Union and the methods employed to ensure passage of the plan for it in the Irish parliament.[31] Collections of essays marking the bicentennial of the Union flesh out the story of both before and after.[32] Worth singling out is Malcomson's distinguished offering on the fortunes of the Irish representative peers who sat in the new United Kingdom House of Lords – and also on their eventual demise.[33]

The eighteenth-century penal laws targeting Roman Catholics are dealt with in two very different essay collections. *Catholic Ireland*, Maureen Wall's collected essays, brings together the thoughts of a recognized authority on them.[34] *Endurance and emergence*, on the other hand, brings together contributions from a number of different contributors.[35] A short *aperçu* from Cullen is a helpful introduction[36] and Fagan's volume on the oaths required to be taken by those seeking fuller citizenship is also of assistance.[37] McGrath has paid particular attention to the adoption of one of the earliest penal law measures, the statute of 1695,[38] and O'Flaherty has dealt with one aspect of their eventual abolition.[39]

with the Irish politics of the eighteenth century deserving notice include: E. Magennis, *The Irish political system, 1740–1765: the golden age of undertakers* (Dublin, 2000); P. McNally, *Parties, patriots and undertakers* (Dublin, 1997); D. Lammey, 'The growth of the patriot opposition in Ireland during the 1770s', *Parliamentary History*, 7 (1988), 257; D. Kennedy, 'The Irish opposition, parliamentary reform and public opinion, 1792–1794', *Eighteenth-Century Ireland*, 7 (1992), 95. See, too, W.J. McCormack, 'Vision and revision in the study of eighteenth century Irish parliament rhetoric', *Eighteenth-Century Ireland*, 2 (1987), 7.

30 G.C. Bolton, *The passing of the Irish Act of Union* (Oxford, 1966).
31 P.M. Geoghegan, *The Irish Act of Union: a study in high politics, 1798–1801* (Dublin 1999).
32 'Essays on the British-Irish Union of 1801', *TRHS*, 6th series, 10 (2000), 167–408; M. Brown, P.M. Geoghegan and J. Kelly (eds), *The Irish Act of Union: bicentennial essays* (Dublin, 2003).
33 'The Irish peerage and the Union, 1800–1971', *TRHS*, 6th series, 10 (2000), 289.
34 M. Wall, *Catholic Ireland in the eighteenth century, collected essays*, edited by G. O'Brien (Dublin, 1989).
35 T.P. Power and K. Whelan (eds), *Endurance and emergence: Catholics in Ireland in the eighteenth century* (Dublin, 1990).
36 L. Cullen, 'Catholics under the penal law', *Eighteenth-Century Ireland*, 1 (1986), 23.
37 P. Fagan, *Divided loyalties: the question of the oath for Irish Catholics in the eighteenth century* (Dublin, 1997).
38 C.I. McGrath, 'Securing the Protestant interest: the origins and purpose of the penal laws of 1695', *IHS*, 30 (1996), 25.
39 E. O'Flaherty, 'Ecclesiastical politics and the dismantling of the penal laws in Ireland', *IHS*, 26 (1988), 33.

Miscellaneous constitutional topics are dealt with by a variety of authors: the origins of habeas corpus in Ireland by Costello;[40] martial law in Ireland by Keane;[41] the status of acts of the Irish parliament in England by Baker;[42] the legacy of William Molyneux to Irish constitutional thought by Kelly;[43] the failure of the Irish parliament to enact a Bill of Rights in the 1690s, and facets of constitutional integration with England after 1800 by Osborough;[44] problems in administering the extended franchise after 1832 by Greer;[45] the nineteenth-century Party Procession Acts by Maddox and Farrell;[46] the preoccupation with human rights in the drafting of home rule measures by Jaconelli;[47] the Easter Rising courts-martial of 1916 by Barton;[48] the passport controversy and allied difficulties following the creation of the Irish Free State by O'Grady, Macmillan and Daly;[49] the regulation of public dancing (no less) in the 1930s by Austin;[50] opposition on the part of women to the terms of the draft Constitution of 1937 by Luddy;[51] and the role of the Jesuits in the production of that

---

40 See K. Costello, *The law of habeas corpus in Ireland* (Dublin, 2006).
41 R. Keane, 'The will of the general: martial law in Ireland 1535–1924', *IJ*, 25–27 (1990–2), 150.
42 J.H. Baker, 'United and knit to the imperial crown: an English view of the Anglo-Hibernian constitution in 1670' in †Greer and Dawson (eds), *Mysteries*, as in fn. 22, p. 73.
43 P. Kelly, 'William Molyneux and the spirit of liberty in eighteenth-century Ireland', *Eighteenth-Century Ireland*, 3 (1988), 133.
44 W.N. Osborough, 'The failure to enact an Irish bill of rights: a gap in Irish constitutional history', *IJ*, 33 (1998), 392; 'Constitutionally constructing a sense of oneness: facets of law in Ireland after the Union', *IJ*, 37 (2002), 227.
45 D. Greer, 'Lawyers or politicians? The Irish judges and the right to vote, 1832–1850' in Costello (ed.), *Four Courts*, as in fn. 12, p. 126.
46 N.P. Maddox, 'A melancholy record: the story of the nineteenth-century Irish Party Processions Act', *IJ*, 39 (2004), 243; S. Farrell, 'Recapturing the flag: the campaign to repeal the Party Processions Act, 1860–72', *Éire-Ireland*, 32 (2 & 3) (1997), 52. And note, too, C. Kinealy, 'A right to march? The conflict at Dolly's Brae' in D.G. Boyce and R. Swift (eds), *Problems and perspectives in Irish history since 1800: essays in honour of Patrick Buckland* (Dublin, 2004), p. 54.
47 J. Jaconelli, 'Human rights guarantees and Irish home rule', *IJ*, 25–27 (1990–2), 181.
48 B. Barton, *From behind a closed door: secret court-martial records of the 1916 Easter Rising* (Belfast, 2002).
49 J.P. O'Grady, 'The Irish Free State passport and the question of Irish citizenship 1921–4', *IHS*, 26 (1989); 396; G. Macmillan, 'British subjects and Irish citizens: the passport controversy 1923–24', *Éire-Ireland*, 26 (3) (1991), 25; M. Daly, 'Irish nationality and citizenship since 1922', *IHS*, 32 (2001), 377.
50 V.A. Austin, 'The ceili and the Public Dance Halls Act 1935', *Éire-Ireland*, 23 (3) (1993), 7.
51 M. Luddy, 'A sinister and retrogressive proposal: Irish women's opposition to the 1937 draft Constitution', *TRHS*, 6th series, 15 (2005), 175.

document by Faughnan.[52] Diplomatic problems caused by the conviction for terrorism of a man better known as an author and playwright – Brendan Behan – have been analysed;[53] as has the more general question of political extremism and of how to combat it.[54]

Local government in eighteenth-century Limerick is examined by O'Flaherty.[55] Crossman offers a more detailed view for the entire country in the nineteenth century.[56] Reform of the poor law at that time thrust fresh tasks on that level of government, matters considered by both Burke and O'Brien.[57] Kelly, for his part, has studied comparable problems for a crucial period late in the eighteenth century.[58]

2.4 THE COURTS

Here a major gap was plugged with the publication of Crawford's magisterial account of Castle Chamber.[59] Crawford had earlier published a short piece on the court[60] which made a pleasing companion for Wood's original survey back in 1914.[61] *A star chamber court in Ireland* breaks fresh ground, charting the fortunes of this key prerogative tribunal under successive chief governors from Henry Sydney in the reign of Elizabeth I down to Thomas Wentworth in that of Charles I. Throughout, the political background against which Castle Chamber operated is admirably sketched. One appendix sets out in detailed form the entries in the single surviving decree book previously edited for the

---

52 S. Faughnan, 'The Jesuits and the drafting of the Irish constitution of 1937', *IHS*, 26 (1988), 79.

53 C. Holmes, 'The British government and Brendan Behan, 1941–1952: the persistence of the Prevention of Violence Act', *Saothar*, 14 (1989), 125.

54 B. Kissane, 'Defending democracy? The legislative response to political extremism in the Irish Free State, 1922–39', *IHS*, 34 (2004), 156.

55 E. O'Flaherty, 'Urban politics and municipal reform in Limerick, 1723–62', *Eighteenth-Century Ireland*, 6 (1991), 105.

56 V. Crossman, *Local government in nineteenth-century Ireland* (Belfast, 1994).

57 H. Burke, *The people and the poor law in nineteenth-century Ireland* (Dublin, 1987); G. O'Brien, 'The new Poor Law in pre-Famine Ireland: a case history', *IESH*, 12 (1985), 33.

58 J. Kelly, 'Scarcity and poor relief in eighteenth-century Ireland: the subsistence crisis of 1782–4', *IHS*, 28 (1992), 38.

59 †J.G. Crawford, *A star chamber court in Ireland – the court of Castle Chamber, 1571–1641* (Dublin, 2005).

60 'The origins of the castle chamber: a star chamber jurisdiction in Ireland', *AJLH*, 26 (1980), 22.

61 H. Wood, 'The court of castle chamber or star chamber of Ireland', *PRIA*, 32 (1914), section C, 170.

Historical Manuscripts Commission in 1905. Another appendix publishes for the first time a set of precedents prepared for Lord Deputy Wentworth in the 1630s, and which helps to flesh out the story of the court after 1621 when the decree book ends.

The salved Chancery pleadings from the reigns of Elizabeth I and James I had previously attracted the attention of Nicholls.[62] From a somewhat different angle – the study of women as litigants in Chancery – these pleadings have now been skilfully mined by O'Dowd.[63] Ohlmeyer, for her part, has also furnished a preliminary report on the records of Chancery for the early years of the reign of Charles I.[64]

Church courts up to the seventeenth century constitute the focus of a survey authored by Osborough,[65] whilst the Irish court of Admiralty set up in 1570 has an outing at the hands of Costello,[66] from whom further insight into the workings of this (unusually for Ireland) well-documented court can be expected in the future, as well as at those of Appleby and O'Dowd.[67] The Irish House of Lords occupied the pinnacle of the Irish legal system from 1783 to 1800, following the restoration of its appellate jurisdiction – an epoch in the history of the parliamentary upper chamber now visited by Lyall.[68]

Ireland's manor courts were finally ended in the middle of the nineteenth century. A single manor court in the seventeenth century is

---

62 K. Nicholls, 'A calendar of salved Chancery pleadings concerning County Louth', *JLAS*, 17 (1972), 250; 18 (1973), 112.
63 M. O'Dowd, 'Women and the Irish chancery court in the late sixteenth and early seventeenth centuries', *IHS*, 31 (1999), 472.
64 J. Ohlmeyer, 'Records of the Irish court of Chancery: a preliminary report for 1627 to 1634' in †Greer and Dawson (eds), *Mysteries*, as in fn. 22, p. 15.
65 W.N. Osborough, 'Ecclesiastical law and the Reformation in Ireland' in R.H. Helmholz (ed.), *Canon law in Protestant lands* (= Comparative Studies in Continental and Anglo-American Legal History, 11) (Berlin, 1992), 223; reprinted in idem, *Studies*, as in fn. 7, p. 127.
66 K. Costello, 'Sir William Petty and the court of Admiralty in Restoration Ireland' in †P. Brand, K. Costello and W.N. Osborough (eds), *Adventures of the law: proceedings of the 16th British Legal History Conference, Dublin, 2003* (Dublin, 2005), p. 106.
67 J. Appleby and M. O'Dowd, 'The Irish Admiralty: its organisation and development c.1570–1640', *IHS*, 24 (1985), 299 and the same authors' 'Cahir O'Doherty and the *Dove* of Cartemyne 1603–4: a sidelight on Gaelic admiralty jurisdiction', *IJ*, 21 (1986), 290.
*Appleby has edited for the Irish Manuscripts Commission, *Calendar of material relating to Ireland from the High Court of Admiralty examinations* (Dublin, 1992). See, too, his 'Merchants and mariners, pirates and privateers: an introductory survey of the records of the High Court of Admiralty as a source for regional maritime history' in M. McCaughan and J. Appleby (eds), *The Irish Sea: aspects of maritime history* (Belfast, 1989), p. 47.
68 A. Lyall, 'The Irish House of Lords as a judicial body, 1783–1800', *IJ*, 28–30 (1993–5), 314.

examined by Gillespie, whilst McMahon relates the fortunes of these courts in the west of Ireland for the last years of their existence.[69] McCabe has also produced fine accounts of petty sessions courts and of assizes again for the first half of the nineteenth century.[70] Two innovations of the nineteenth century – the Court of Appeal in Chancery and the Landed Estates Court (the successor to the Incumbered Estates Court) – have been expertly analysed by Dowling in articles that represent a major contribution to our understanding of legal changes in mid-Victorian Ireland.[71] Two further innovations in the nineteenth century, the establishment of the Court for Crown Cases Reserved and the creation of the resident magistracy, are the subject of fine studies by Greer and Bonsall respectively.[72]

In the early twentieth century the movement for Irish independence culminated in the establishment in the south of the country in 1922 of the Irish Free State. Prior to then, Sinn Féin, however, had resolved on the erection of a set of courts to replace the crown court system – the so-called 'republican' or Dáil courts. Earlier short articles dealing with these courts[73] have now been superseded by a major survey from Kotsonouris.[74]

69 R. Gillespie, 'A manor court in seventeenth-century Ireland', *IESH*, 25 (1998), 81; R. McMahon, 'Manor courts in the west of Ireland before the Famine' in †Greer and Dawson (eds), *Mysteries*, as in fn. 22, p. 115.

70 D. McCabe, 'Magistrates, peasants and the petty session courts, Mayo, 1823–50', *Cathair na Mart: Journal of the Westport Historical Society*, 5 (1985), 45; 'That part that laws or kings can cause or cure: crown prosecution and jury trial at Longford assizes, 1830–45' in R. Gillespie and G. Moran (eds), *Longford: essays in county history* (Dublin, 1991), p. 153. See, too, McCabe's 'Open court: law and the expansion of magisterial jurisdiction at petty sessions in nineteenth-century Ireland' in †Dawson (ed.), *Reflections*, as in fn. 27, p. 126, and R. McMahon, 'The court of petty sessions and the law in pre-Famine Galway' in R. Gillespie (ed.), *The remaking of modern Ireland 1750–1950: Beckett prize essays in Irish history* (Dublin, 2004), p. 101.

71 J.A. Dowling, 'The Irish Court of Appeal in Chancery 1857–77', *Journal of Legal History*, 21 (2000), 83; 'The Landed Estates Court, Ireland', *Journal of Legal History*, 26 (2005), 143. See, too, M.C. Lyons, *Illustrated incumbered estates: Ireland, 1850–1905 – lithographic and other illustrative material in the incumbered estates rentals* (Whitegate, Co. Clare, 1993).

72 D. Greer, 'A security against illegality? The reservation of crown cases in nineteenth-century Ireland' in †Dawson (ed.), *Reflections*, as in fn. 27, p. 163; P. Bonsall, *The Irish RMs: the resident magistrates in the British administration of Ireland* (Dublin, n.d. [1997]).

73 C. Maguire, 'The Republican courts', *Capuchin Annual* (1969), 378; J. Casey, 'The Republican courts in Ireland 1919–22', *IJ*, 5 (1970), 322; idem, 'The genesis of the Dáil courts', *IJ*, 9 (1974), 326; F. Costello, 'The Republican courts and the decline of British rule in Ireland, 1919–21', *Éire-Ireland*, 25 (2) (1990), 36.

74 M. Kotsonouris, *Retreat from revolution: the Dáil courts, 1920–24* (Dublin, 1994). And see, too, H. Laird, *Subversive law in Ireland, 1879–1920: from unwritten law to the Dáil courts* (Dublin, 2005).

The same author has also examined in equal depth the work of the special commission that was set up to deal with unfinished business after the new Irish government ended the Dáil courts, deciding rather to adopt – and adapt – the crown court system.[75]

The Anglo-Irish treaty of 1921 provided for the continuation of appeals from the new Irish state to the Judicial Committee of the Privy Council in London. Retention of this avenue of appeal was unpopular in political circles and the appeal itself was eventually abolished by statute in the 1930s. The saga that led to the ending of the appeal has been revisited by Mohr.[76] The contemporary Irish Supreme Court is restricted to handing down unanimous judgments on constitutional references. This 'one-judgment' rule has been considered by Keane, the recently retired chief justice.[77]

2.5 SUBSTANTIVE LAW

2.5.1 Ecclesiastical law

Doctrinal developments in this branch of law have generated little interest despite the significant role occupied by the church courts and (in Irish terms) the comparative abundance of surviving source-material. Pawlisch has, however, traversed difficult terrain to explain the *Case of proxies*, an early seventeenth-century adjudication reported in Davies' *Reports*.[78] Bric has furnished a guide to the law on tithe in the eighteenth century,[79] and difficulties encountered in the previous century in record-keeping by the senior court, that of the Prerogative and Faculties, are covered by Osborough.[80]

---

75 †M. Kotsonouris, *The winding-up of the Dáil courts, 1922–1925: an obvious duty* (Dublin, 2004).
76 T. Mohr, 'Law without loyalty – the abolition of the Irish appeal to the Privy Council', *IJ*, 37 (2002), 187. See, too, his 'Salmon of knowledge' [a discussion of brehon law evidence tendered in a key related 1930s lawsuit], in *Peritia*, 16 (2002), 360.
77 R. Keane, 'The one judgment rule in the Supreme Court' in †Dawson (ed.), *Reflections*, as in fn. 27, p. 307.
78 H.S. Pawlisch, 'Sir John Davies' law reports and the Case of Proxies', *IJ*, 17 (1982), 368.
79 M.J. Bric, 'The tithe system in eighteenth century Ireland', *PRIA*, 86 (1986), section C, 271.
80 W.N. Osborough, 'Wills that go missing: the quest for the last testament of Christopher Wandesford, lord deputy of Ireland, 1640' in †Dawson (ed.), *Reflections*, as in fn. 27, p. 1. Another volume of abstracts of wills has also appeared: **Registry of Deeds Dublin, Abstracts of wills, vol. 3: 1785–1832*, ed. E. Ellis and P. Beryl Eustace (Dublin, 1984).

From the late medieval and early modern periods three further Armagh registers have made it into recent editions: the registers associated with the archiepiscopates of Swetman, 1361–80; Fleming, 1404–16; and Octavian de Palatio, 1478–1513. The last of these, produced in a two-volume edition by Sughi,[81] is of most interest here. A feature of the second volume is the index of selected subjects and procedures which facilitates the quick finding of entries in the register on such matters as papal judges delegate, exercising functions in Ireland which, of course, terminated at the Reformation.

In the late nineteenth century the disciplining of a Roman Catholic priest, the Revd O'Keeffe, the parish priest of Callan, Co. Kilkenny, by his ecclesiastical superiors provoked a sensational defamation suit – and two works of modern fiction. The dispute, touching as it did on church-state relations, has been re-examined by Osborough.[82] A little earlier, a rather different controversy again troubled church-state relations: the refusal of the authorities at lunatic asylums in Ulster to sanction the appointment of chaplains. This bizarre controversy also ended up in court; it, too, has recently been reinvestigated.[83]

2.5.2 Law of property

In his invaluable *Landlords and tenants in mid-Victorian Ireland*,[84] Vaughan furnishes the background for an understanding of a large number of problems linked to land ownership and use in the century.[85] Vaughan had previously examined evictions in Co. Donegal;[86] Yager has now dealt likewise with earlier evictions on the Mullet peninsula in

---

81 *Registrum Octaviani alias Liber niger: the register of Octavian de Palatio, archbishop of Armagh, 1478–1513*, 2 vols. (Dublin, 1999). See, too, M.A. Sughi, 'The appointment of Octavian de Palatio as archbishop of Armagh, 1477–8', *IHS*, 31 (1998), 145.
82 W.N. Osborough, 'Another country, other days: revisiting Thomas Kilroy's "The big chapel"', *Irish University Review*, 32 (2002), 34. See *O'Keeffe v. Cardinal Cullen* (1873) IR 7 CL 319.
83 P. Prior and D. Griffiths, 'The chaplaincy question – The lord lieutenant v. The Belfast lunatic asylum', *Éire-Ireland*, 32 (2&3) (1997), 137. The resultant lawsuit is reported as *The Queen (Carroll) v. Belfast District Lunatic Asylum* (1851) 5 ICLR 375. For a general history of mental illness in the country, see J. Robins, *Fools and mad: a history of the insane in Ireland* (Dublin, 1986).
84 W.E. Vaughan, *Landlords and tenants in mid-Victorian Ireland* (Oxford, 1994).
85 Land law problems and the rural landlord-tenant relationship are also discussed in Brady, 'Legal developments', as in fn. 14. L.M. Geary, *The plan of campaign, 1886–91* (Cork, 1986), is also helpful for context.
86 W.E. Vaughan, *Sin, sheep and Scotsmen: John George Adair and the Derryveagh evictions, 1861* (Belfast, 1983).

Co. Mayo.[87] Incumbrances form part of the historical background as well, and presented challenges for the Landed Estates Court, as Dowling, in an article previously referred to,[88] proceeds to explain. They are touched on as well in Curtis' survey of landlord responses to a key event of the late nineteenth century, the Land War.[89]

Essays in a collection, produced to coincide with the one-hundred-and-fiftieth anniversary of the Law Faculty at Queen's University Belfast,[90] explore, in a historical context, a range of issues in the Irish law of property: distress for non-payment of rent (Alan Dowling); the durability of conacre (David Moore); the Irish wife's property rights (Sheena Grattan); the law on rights of way (Norma Dawson). Dowling, the first of the authors mentioned in this collection, has also explored the origins of Deasy's Act and of land registration and the question of succession to the Hertford Irish estates in the 1870s.[91] Power has investigated the origins of the Irish doctrine of graft[92] and Bull has surveyed political nationalism's response to the Land Act of 1903.[93] Protection for town tenants was introduced by legislation early in the twentieth century; earlier conflict has been researched by Graham and Hood.[94]

Irish land law has been heavily influenced by the land law of England, but differences emerged and these remain. These differences are critically examined by Wylie in an article which addresses the important theme of the Irishness of the home-grown product.[95]

---

87 T. Yager, 'Mass eviction in the Mullet peninsula during and after the Great Famine', *IESH*, 23 (1996), 24.
88 Above, fn. 71.
89 L. Perry Curtis, Jr, 'Landlord responses to the Irish land war 1877–1887', *Éire-Ireland*, 38 (3&4) (2003), 134.
90 N. Dawson, D. Greer and P. Ingram (eds), *One hundred and fifty years of Irish law* (Belfast, Dublin, 1996).
91 A. Dowling, 'The genesis of Deasy's Act', *NILQ*, 40 (1989), 53; 'Of ships and sealing wax; the introduction of land registration in Ireland', *NILQ*, 44 (1993), 360; 'Under which King, Bezonian? Succession to the Hertford Irish estates in 1870', *NILQ*, 49 (1998), 267.
92 A. Power, 'The eighteenth-century origins of the Irish doctrine of graft' in O. Breen, J. Casey and A. Kerr (eds), *Liber memorialis, Professor James C. Brady* (Dublin, 2001), p. 326.
93 P. Bull, 'The significance of the nationalist response to the Irish land act of 1903', *IHS*, 28 (1993), 283.
94 B.J. Graham and S. Hood, 'Town tenant protest in late nineteenth and early twentieth century Ireland', *IESH*, 21 (1994), 39.
95 J.C.W. Wylie, 'The Irishness of Irish land law', *NILQ*, 46 (1995), 332.

2.5.3 Labour law

Past industrial conflict has been the focus of a couple of essays in *Saothar*, the journal of the Irish Labour History Society: industrial violence in late eighteenth-century Dublin (Brian Henry);[96] conflict among colliers and quarrymen in the early nineteenth century in Co. Tipperary (Des Cowman).[97] O'Connor, as well as furnishing a history of labour in Ireland, 1824–1960, has also written of Luddite activity in the early nineteenth century.[98] Abuses of the Truck Acts in Co. Donegal later in the century are considered by Greer,[99] who also, in collaboration with Nicolson, has furnished a major review of the operation of a legislative code of immediate interest to the industrial worker – the Factories Acts.[100] Chapter 11 in this magisterial volume examines the use made of the criminal law in enforcing the code, whilst chapter 12 explores the development in Ireland of private law remedies made possible by employers' liability,[101] a particularly welcome bonus since the development of such remedies, via tort law in general, has attracted scant interest.[102] The work of women factory inspectors – touched on by Greer and Nicolson – is examined in greater depth by McFeely in a book, three of whose chapters concentrate on Ireland.[103]

A collection of documents illustrative of the growth of Irish labour has made a welcome appearance.[104] Diplomatic tangles over unemploy-

---

96 'Industrial violence, combinations and the law in late eighteenth-century Dublin', *Saothar*, 18 (1993), 19.
97 'Combination, conflict and control: colliers and quarrymen in Tipperary, 1825–45', *Saothar*, 26 (2001), 27.
98 E. O'Connor, *A labour history of Ireland, 1824–1960* (Dublin 1992); 'Active sabotage in industrial conflict, 1817–23', *IESH*, 12 (1985), 51.
99 D. Greer, 'Middling hard on coin: truck in Donegal in the 1890s' in †Dawson (ed.), *Reflections*, as in fn. 27, p. 278.
100 †D. Greer and J.W. Nicolson, *The Factory Acts in Ireland, 1802–1914* (Dublin, 2002).
101 Also examined by Greer in his article, 'A false mawkish and mongrel humanity? The early history of employers' liability in Ireland' in Breen, Casey and Kerr (eds), *Liber memorialis*, as in fn. 92, p. 227.
102 One exception is furnished by W.N. Osborough in an examination of doctrinal developments in negligence triggered by tramway accidents: 'Recollection of things past – trams, their clientele and the law', *NILQ*, 46 (1995), 443. The same author has examined an amount of modern private law litigation in Ireland where Roman law authority was opened: see 'Roman law in Ireland', *IJ*, 25–27 (1990–2), 212, reprinted idem, *Studies*, as in fn. 7, p. 11.
103 M. Drake McFeely, *Lady inspectors: the campaign for a better workplace, 1893–1921* (Oxford, 1998).
104 *Workers in union: documents and commentaries on the history of Irish labour*, ed. Fergus A. D'Arcy and K. Hannigan (Dublin, 1988).

ment insurance between the Republic and Britain in the twentieth century sound an appropriate contemporary note.[105]

2.5.4 Commercial law

Commercial credit in earlier days was arranged through a system of statute staples. Statute staple books for Ireland in the seventeenth century have now been edited by Ohlmeyer and Ó Ciardha,[106] and Ohlmeyer has elsewhere explained their historical significance and value.[107] Ollerenshaw has produced a major text on the history of banking in Ulster[108] which, in one sense, brings the story of arranging credit up to date. Dudley has published two fine studies on the origins of insurance practice in Dublin,[109] and Osborough has re-examined key decisions of the early 1920s on the interpretation of the phrase 'civil commotion' in exception clauses in insurance contracts.[110]

2.5.5 Procedure and evidence

Jury trial and other aspects of procedure in criminal cases have been explored by David Johnson,[111] whilst Jackson has revisited the united Irish opposition to what became for England and Wales the Criminal Evidence Act 1898.[112] A lacuna in our understanding of civil procedure has been admirably filled by Greer who has delved into the origins of the Irish civil bill.[113]

---

105 J.B. Wolf, 'Withholding their due: the dispute between Ireland and Great Britain over unemployment insurance payments to conditionally landed Irish wartime volunteer workers', *Saothar*, 21 (1996), 39.

106 *The Irish statute staple books, 1596–1687*, ed. J. Ohlmeyer and E. Ó Ciardha (Dublin, 1998).

107 *IESH*, 27 (2000), 63.

108 P. Ollerenshaw, *The Belfast banks, 1825–1914* (Manchester, 1987).

109 R. Dudley, 'The rise of the annuity company in Dublin 1700–1800', *IESH*, 29 (2002), 1; 'Fire insurance in Dublin, 1700–1860', *IESH*, 30 (2003), 24. See, too, R.S. Harrison, *Irish insurance: historical perspectives, 1650–1939* (Cork, 1992).

110 W.N. Osborough, 'Forcibly commandeered transport and owner's insurance: the deciding of two test cases in the 1920s', *IJ*, 11 (1976), 105; reprinted in idem, *Studies*, as in fn. 7, p. 296.

111 D.S. Johnson, 'Trial by jury in Ireland, 1869–1914', *Journal of Legal History*, 17 (1996), 270; 'The trials of Sam Gray: Monaghan politics and nineteenth-century Irish criminal procedure', *IJ*, 20 (1985), 109.

112 C. Jackson, 'Irish political opposition to the passage of reform, 1883–98: the Criminal Evidence Act 1898' in J.F. McEldowney and P. O'Higgins (eds), *The common law tradition* (Dublin, 1990), p. 185.

113 D.S. Greer, 'The development of civil bill procedure in Ireland' in McEldowney and O'Higgins (eds), *The common law*, as in fn. 112, p. 27.

2.6 ADMINISTRATION OF CRIMINAL JUSTICE

Criminal justice and its administration, together with the social background against which criminality in Ireland needs to be understood, have generated a great deal of interest among writers and researchers. *Albion's fatal tree: crime and society in eighteenth-century England*, the remarkable assemblage of pioneering studies for England published in 1975,[114] furnished the incentive for Irish historians to repeat the exercise for Ireland. The first major monograph to enter the field, from Garnham, is an impressive résumé for the period from 1692 to 1760.[115] Mining an unusual array of sources, Garnham convinces with his survey, but the lack of Irish law reports until the end of the eighteenth century places all researchers at something of a disadvantage. Garnham's follow-up essay, 'How violent was eighteenth-century Ireland',[116] is another well-argued offering and, again, no less potentially provocative; it keeps company, therefore, with the writings of Connolly on a broadly similar theme.[117]

Garnham has revisited a number of individual *causes célèbres* from the eighteenth century – Paul Farrell, James Cotter and Lord Santry.[118] Other authors have adopted a similar approach: Morgan in his account of the proceedings against the Gaelic chieftain, Brian O'Rourke, in the

114 D. Hay, P. Linebaugh, J.G. Rule, E.P. Thompson and C. Winslow (eds), *Albion's fatal tree: crime and society in eighteenth-century England* (London, 1975).
115 N. Garnham, *The courts, crime and the criminal law in Ireland, 1692–1760* (Dublin, 1996). See, too, his 'Criminal legislation in the Irish parliament, 1692–1760' in Hayton (ed.), *Irish parliament*, as in fn. 27, p. 55.
116 N. Garnham, 'How violent was eighteenth-century Ireland?', *IHS*, 30 (1997), 377.
117 S.J. Connolly, 'Violence and order in the eighteenth century' in P. O'Flanagan, P. Ferguson and Kevin Whelan (eds), *Rural Ireland: modernisation and change* (Cork, 1985), p. 42; 'Albion's fatal twigs: justice and law in the eighteenth century' in R. Mitchison and P. Roebuck (eds), *Economy and society in Scotland and Ireland, 1500–1939* (Edinburgh, 1955), p. 117; 'The Houghers' in C.H.E. Philpin (ed.), *Nationalism and popular protest in early eighteenth-century Ireland* (Cambridge, 1987), p. 139; 'Law, order and popular protest in early eighteenth-century Ireland: the case of the Houghers' in P.J. Corish (ed.), *Radicals, rebels and establishments* (Historical Studies, XV) (Belfast, 1985), p. 51; *Religion, law and power: the making of Protestant Ireland, 1660–1760* (Oxford, 1995), p. 198. Gillespie has covered one facet of the crime problem in an earlier century: R.G. Gillespie, 'Women and crime in seventeenth-century Ireland' in M. MacCurtain and M. O'Dowd (eds), *Women in early modern Ireland* (Edinburgh, 1991), p. 43.
118 'The short career of Paul Farrell: a brief consideration of law enforcement in eighteenth-century Dublin', *Eighteenth-Century Ireland*, 11 (1996), 46; 'The trials of James Cotter and Henry, Baron Barry of Santry: two case studies in the administration of criminal justice in early eighteenth-century Ireland', *IHS*, 31 (1999), 328.

reign of Elizabeth I;[119] Hart in his account of the fate of 'fighting Fitzgerald' at the end of the eighteenth century;[120] Holloway in his commemoration of the State trial of Daniel O'Connell; Kostel on the prosecution of the Dublin Fenians in 1865–6;[121] and Bourke on the fall-out from the burning alive of Bridget Cleary at the end of the nineteenth century.[122] Henry has edited a pamphlet of the 1760s that addressed itself to the problem of street crime,[123] and Osborough has reproduced the text of a rare judgment of the Irish King's Bench handed down in 1739 which dealt with the distinction between murder and manslaughter.[124]

Some writers have concentrated their energies on writing about particular forms of criminal behaviour. Gibbons has explored the phenomenon of the sending of threatening letters in the half-century before the Famine[125] and Lapoint Ireland's comparative immunity from the persecution of witches over the centuries.[126] Kelly has been the most prolific. Apart from his full-length book on duelling,[127] there are shorter contributions on rape, infanticide and the abduction of heiresses.[128] For good measure, Kelly has also published a collection of speeches from condemned prisoners – speeches from the gallows.[129] Very different in subject-matter, Malcolm's revisiting of

---

119 H. Morgan, 'Extradition and treason-trial of a Gaelic lord: the case of Brian O'Rourke', *IJ*, 22 (1987), 285.

120 A.R. Hart, 'Fighting Fitzgerald – mad, bad and dangerous to know: an eighteenth-century murder trial', *NILQ*, 49 (1998), 221.

121 I. Holloway, '*O'Connell v. The Queen*: a sesquicentennial remembrance', *NILQ*, 46 (1995), 63; R.W. Kostel, 'Rebels in the dock: the prosecution of the Dublin Fenians, 1865–6', *Éire-Ireland*, 34 (2) (1999), 70.

122 A. Bourke, *The burning of Bridget Cleary: a true story* (London, 1999).

123 'Animadversions on the street robberies in Dublin, 1765', ed. B. Henry, *IJ*, 23 (1988), 347.

124 W.N. Osborough, 'Murder or manslaughter: a 1739 decision of the Irish King's Bench', *IJ*, 39 (2004), 275.

125 S.R. Gibbons, *Captain Rock, night errant: the threatening letters of pre-Famine Ireland, 1801–45* (Dublin, 2004).

126 E.C. Lapoint, 'Irish immunity to witch-hunting 1534–1711', *Éire-Ireland*, 27 (2) (1992), 76.

127 J. Kelly, *That damn'd thing called honour: duelling in Ireland, 1570–1800* (Cork, 1995).

128 'A most inhuman and barbarous piece of villainy: an exploration of the crime of rape in eighteenth-century Ireland', *Eighteenth-Century Ireland*, 10 (1995), 78; 'Infanticide in eighteenth-century Ireland', *IESH*, 19 (1992), 5; 'The abduction of women of fortune in eighteenth-century Ireland', *Eighteenth-Century Ireland*, 9 (1994), 7. See, too, here: A.P.W. Malcomson, *The pursuit of the heiress: aristocratic marriage in Ireland, 1750–1820* (Belfast, 1982).

129 J. Kelly, *Gallows speeches from eighteenth-century Ireland* (Dublin, 2001).

the controversy over the Contagious Diseases Acts brings us well into the nineteenth century.[130]

Agrarian unrest had previously generated a small literature. Important additions continue to be made. A general survey is furnished by a collection of essays edited by Clark and Donnelly.[131] There are also a number of surveys more limited in scope. Magennis returns to the 'Hearts of Oak' disturbances in Ulster in the 1760s,[132] whilst O'Hanrahan focuses on the struggle over tithe in Kilkenny in the early 1830s,[133] Malcolm on 'the reign of terror' in Carlow in the later 1830s,[134] and Beames on peasant assassination in Tipperary in the 1830s and '40s.[135] Crossman attempts an overview covering the years between 1821 and 1841.[136] The burning of Wildgoose Lodge in Co. Louth in the second decade of the nineteenth century, which had already attracted a great deal of scholarly attention, has seen its bibliography extended.[137]

Twentieth-century rural delinquency has manifested itself in rather different ways, the political border between Northern Ireland and the Irish Republic being on some occasions at least to blame, as Johnson explained in a pioneering effort on cattle smuggling.[138]

Politically inspired violence has witnessed substantial additions to the pre-existing literature. The eighteenth century has been examined from this perspective by Connolly in an article linking Jacobites, Whiteboys and Republicans.[139] Townsend has furnished an overview of

---

130 E. Malcolm, 'Troops of largely diseased women: VD, the Contagious Diseases Acts and moral policing in late nineteenth-century Ireland', *IESH*, 26 (1991), 1.
131 S. Clark and J.S. Donnelly, Jr (eds), *Irish peasants: violence and political unrest, 1780–1914* (Madison, Wis, Manchester, 1987). See, too, the writings of Connolly, as in fn. 117.
132 E.F. Magennis, 'A Presbyterian insurrection? Reconsidering the Hearts of Oak disturbances of July 1763', *IHS*, 31 (1998), 165.
133 M. O'Hanrahan, 'The tithe war in Co. Kilkenny 1830–34' in W. Nolan and K. Whelan (eds), *Kilkenny: history and society* (Dublin, 1990), p. 481.
134 E. Malcolm, 'The reign of terror in Carlow: the politics of policing in Ireland in the late 1830s', *IHS*, 32 (2000), 59.
135 M.R. Beames, 'Rural conflict in pre-Famine Ireland: peasant assassination in Tipperary, 1837–47' in C.H.E. Philpin (ed.), *Nationalism and popular protest in Ireland* (Cambridge, 1987), p. 280.
136 V. Crossman, 'Emergency legislation and agrarian disorder in Ireland, 1821–41', *IHS*, 27 (1991), 309.
137 R. Ó Muirí, 'The burning of Wildgoose Lodge', *JLAS*, 21 (1985–8), 117. To be read in conjunction with earlier articles in the same journal on the same topic – by T.G.F. Paterson in *JLAS*, 12 (1949–52), 159, and by D.J. Casey in *JLAS*, 18 (1974), 140.
138 D.S. Johnson, 'Cattle smuggling on the Irish border, 1932–38', *IESH*, 7 (1979), 41.
139 S.J. Connolly, 'Jacobites, Whiteboys and Republicans: varieties of disaffection in

the problem in its entirety from the time of the Young Irelanders down to the present day.[140] More confined in its focus is Hirst's book on religion, politics and violence in Belfast in the nineteenth century.[141]

The linkage between moral reform and social control (and thus prevention of the descent into criminality) has been considered in two somewhat different contexts: by D'Arcy in the context of the abolition of Donnybrook Fair in Dublin[142] and by Hempton and Hill in that of the rise of evangelical Protestantism in Ulster.[143] Crime prevention *simpliciter* in the nineteenth century is examined by Griffin.[144]

Two of the essays listed above – Garnham on the question of violence in eighteenth-century Ireland (above, fn. 116) and Kelly on the crime of rape in the same century (above, fn. 128) – are reprinted in a collection of essays on Irish criminal justice history brought out by O'Donnell and McAuley.[145] Four further essays reprinted in the same collection deal with aspects of the history of policing: Palmer's 'The Irish police experiment; the beginnings of modern police in the British Isles, 1785–95'; Bridgeman's 'The constabulary and the criminal justice system in nineteenth-century Ireland'; Cochrane's 'The policeman's lot is not a happy one: duty, discipline, pay and conditions in the Dublin Metropolitan Police, *c*.1838–45'; and Lowe's 'Policing famine Ireland'.

A great deal of other work on policing in Ireland has made it into print. Monographs include O'Sullivan's overview of the various Irish constabularies from 1822 to 1922;[146] Griffin's account of the 'Bulkies' of Belfast's local force from 1800 to 1865;[147] Malcolm's social history;[148]

---

eighteenth-century Ireland', *Eighteenth-Century Ireland*, 18 (2001), 63. For other contributions from Connolly, see above fn. 117.

140 C. Townsend, *Political violence in Ireland: government resistance since 1848* (Oxford, 1983). And see, too, the works listed at fnn. 16 and 17 above.

141 C. Hirst, *Religion, politics and violence in nineteenth-century Belfast: the Pound and Sandy Row* (Dublin, 2002).

142 F.A. D'Arcy, 'The decline and fall of Donnybrook Fair: moral reform and social control in nineteenth-century Ireland', *Saothar*, 13 (1988), 7. See, too, S. Ó Maitiú, *The humours of Donnybrook: Dublin's famous fair and its suppression* (Dublin, 1995).

143 D. Hempton and M. Hill, 'Godliness and good citizenship: evangelical Protestantism and social control in Ulster, 1790–1850', *Saothar*, 13 (1988), 68.

144 B. Griffin, 'Prevention and detection of crime in nineteenth-century Ireland' in †Dawson (ed.), *Reflections*, as in fn. 27, p. 99.

145 I. O'Donnell and F. McAuley (eds), *Criminal justice history: themes and controversies from pre-independence Ireland* (Dublin, 2003).

146 D.J. O'Sullivan, *The Irish constabularies, 1822–1922: a century of policing in Ireland* (Dingle, Co. Kerry, 1999).

147 †B. Griffin, *The Bulkies: police and crime in Belfast, 1800–1865* (Dublin, 1997).

148 E. Malcolm, *The Irish policeman, 1822–1922: a life* (Dublin, 2006).

and Palmer's survey of the police and the tackling of protest in both England and Ireland.[149]

Other studies on the police include D'Arcy and Lowe on police unrest in 1882,[150] Lowe alone on the war against the Royal Irish Constabulary, 1919–21,[151] Federowicz on the problems consequent on the RIC's disbandment in 1922,[152] and O'Brien on the missing personnel records for the same force.[153] Ball has published the memoirs of a serving RIC officer[154] and Herlihy has produced histories and genealogical data for both the RIC and the Dublin Metropolitan Police.[155]

The same collection of essays assembled by O'Donnell and McAuley[156] reprints four seminal essays on aspects of the history of the Irish penal system. Conveniently brought together therefore the reader will find: Heaney on the fortunes of the Richmond penitentiary in Dublin; Carey on Mountjoy prison also in Dublin; Dooley on the reformer Walter Crofton; and Bretherton on the short-lived inebriate reformatories. Supplementary research is reflected in Carey's subsequent book on Mountjoy[157] and Krause's study of the impact of Crofton's reforms on penal practice in Germany.[158] Associated historical studies encompass Carroll-Burke's monograph on the making of the Irish convict prison[159] and Reece's on transportation of Irish convicts to Australia.[160] Windrum has written on the experience

---

149 S.H. Palmer, *Police and protest in England and Ireland, 1780–1850* (Cambridge, 1998).
150 F. D'Arcy, 'The Dublin police strike of 1882', *Saothar*, 23 (1998), 33; W.J. Lowe, 'The constabulary agitation of 1882', *IHS*, 31 (1998), 37.
151 'The war against the RIC, 1919–21', *Éire-Ireland*, 37 (3&4) (2002), 79.
152 K. Federowicz, 'The problems of disbandment: the RIC and imperial migration, 1919–29', *IHS*, 30 (1996), 88.
153 G. O'Brien, 'The missing personnel records of the RIC', *IHS*, 31 (1999), 505.
154 J. Ball, *A policeman's Ireland: recollections of Samuel Waters, RIC* (Cork, 1999).
155 J. Herlihy, *The Royal Irish Constabulary: a short history and genealogical guide* (Dublin, 1997); *The Royal Irish Constabulary: alphabetical list of officers and men* (Dublin, 1999); *Royal Irish Constabulary officers: a biographical dictionary and genealogical guide, 1816–1922* (Dublin, 2005); *The Dublin Metropolitan Police: a short history and genealogical guide* (Dublin, 2001); *The Dublin Metropolitan Police: alphabetical list of officers and men* (Dublin, 2001).
156 I. O'Donnell and F. Mcauley (eds), *Criminal justice history: themes and controversies from pre-independence Ireland* (Dublin, 2003).
157 T. Carey, *Mountjoy: the story of a prison* (Cork, 2000).
158 †T. Krause, 'The influence of Sir Walter Crofton's Irish System on prison reform in Germany' in Brand, Costello and Osborough (eds), *Adventures*, as in fn. 66, p. 234.
159 P. Carroll-Burke, *Colonial discipline: the making of the Irish convict prison* (Dublin, 2000).
160 B. Reece, *The origins of Irish convict transportation to New South Wales* (Houndmills, 2001).

of prison reform in a single Irish county, Co. Down.[161] A prison diary and prisoners' letters from the early 1920s have also been edited for publication.[162] The story of the prison ship, the *Argenta*, has also been revisited,[163] as have the fortunes of a group of later Irish prisoners.[164] Barnes' book on the origins and development of Ireland's industrial schools filled one very obvious gap, as does O'Brien's long article on capital punishment in independent Ireland.[165]

Finally, note should be taken of Griffin's invaluable guide to sources for the study of crime in Ireland between the Act of Union in 1800 and Irish independence,[166] as well as Conley's short offering on Irish criminal records and Finnane's work on criminal statistics, both for the end of the nineteenth century.[167]

2.7 THE LEGAL PROFESSION

Here Brand provides a link with the medieval period in an account of Irish law students and lawyers on the eve of the modern era.[168] Thereafter, the history of the profession is inextricably linked with the institution of King's Inns, the Irish inn of court, which traces its origins back to the reign of Henry VIII. We are fortunate now to have three volumes by Kenny which tackle aspects of the history of this institution. The first is a straightforward narrative history covering its

161 C. Windrum, 'The provision and practice of prison reform in County Down' in L. Proudfoot (ed.), *Down, history and society* (Dublin, 1997), p. 327.

162 J. Campbell, *As I was among the captives: prison diary, 1922–1923*, ed. E. Ní Chuilleanáin (Cork, 2001); *Prisoners: the Civil War letters of Ernie O'Malley*, ed. R. English and C. O'Malley (Swords, Co. Dublin, 1991).

163 D. Kleinrichert, *Republican imprisonment and the prison ship Argenta* (Dublin, 2000).

164 C. Collette, 'So utterly forgotten: Irish prisoners and the 1924 Labour Government', *North Western Labour History Jl*, 16 (1991–2), 73.

165 J. Barnes, *Irish industrial schools, 1868–1908: origins and development* (Dublin, 1989); G. O'Brien, 'Capital punishment in Ireland, 1922–1964' in †Dawson (ed.), *Reflections*, as in fn. 27, p. 223.

166 B. Griffin, *Sources for the study of crime in Ireland, 1801–1921* (Dublin, 2004).

167 C.A. Conley, 'Irish criminal records, 1865–1892', *Éire-Ireland*, 28 (1) (1993), 97; M. Finnane, 'Irish crime without the outrage: the statistics of criminal justice in the later nineteenth century' in †Dawson (ed.), *Reflections*, as in fn. 27, p. 203. See, too, I. O'Donnell's fascinating historical survey, 'Lethal violence in Ireland, 1841 to 2003', *BJC*, 45 (2005), 671. For details of other published work on facets of criminal justice see above fn. 72 (Greer on criminal appeals), fn. 111 (Johnson on jury trial, etc.) and fn. 112 (Jackson on criminal evidence).

168 P. Brand, 'Irish law students and lawyers in late medieval Ireland', *IHS*, 32 (2000), 161.

origins, its reestablishment in the early 1600s and its subsequent fortunes down to the passing in 1800 of the Act of Union.[169] The second in the trilogy focuses on initiatives taken to promote professional training for barristers in the nineteenth century, initiatives linked to one Tristram Kennedy.[170] Kennedy's brainchild, the Dublin Law Institute, ultimately collapsed, but there was an important sequel dealt with in a separate essay by Kenny.[171] The third volume in the trilogy tackles head-on a controversy involving the benchers of the Inns in the late twentieth century when the decision was reached to sell portion of their library to raise funds for the Inns.[172] (In Scotland, it may be recalled, part of the library of the Faculty of Advocates formed the basis of the National Library of Scotland[173] – no comparable measure to protect the local Inns' cultural heritage seems to have been contemplated.) In a separate essay, Kenny has written about the records held by King's Inns,[174] and Ryan-Smolin, for her part, has furnished an illustrated catalogue of portraits held there too.[175]

Daire Hogan, in a volume that appeared in 1986, also deals with facets of the more modern history of King's Inns.[176] This volume has distinct chapters covering the recent history of Irish barristers and also – this was a first – of Irish solicitors. Four years later a collection of essays included three on attorneys and solicitors,[177] but the lower branch (if this designation, offensive to some, is allowable) is the exclusive concern of a further collection of essays, edited by Hall and Hogan in 2002.[178] The emergence of women in the profession (an essay

---

169 †C. Kenny, *King's Inns and the kingdom of Ireland: the Irish inn of court, 1541–1800* (Dublin, 1992).
170 †*Tristram Kennedy and the revival of Irish legal training, 1835–1885* (Dublin, 1996).
171 C. Kenny, 'Adventures in training: the Irish genesis of the remarkable and far-sighted Select Committee on Legal Education, 1846' in †Brand, Costello and Osborough (eds), *Adventures*, as in fn. 66, p. 289.
172 †*King's Inns and the battle of the books, 1972: cultural controversy at a Dublin library* (Dublin, 2002).
173 See the statute of 1925: 15 & 16 Geo. V, c. 73.
174 'The records of King's Inns' in †D. Hogan and W.N. Osborough (eds), *Brehons, serjeants and attorneys* (Dublin, 1990), p. 231.
175 W. Ryan-Smolin, *King's Inns portraits* (Dublin, 1992).
176 D. Hogan, *The legal profession in Ireland, 1789–1922* (Dublin, 1986).
177 †D. Hogan and W.N. Osborough (eds), *Brehons, serjeants and attorneys* (Dublin, 1990). One of the three (by Osborough) looks at lawyers in the Irish novels of Anthony Trollope, a topic revisited a few years later by P. Ingram: 'Law and lawyers in Trollope's Ireland' in Dawson, Greer and Ingram (eds), *Irish law*, as in fn. 90, p. 125.
178 E.G. Hall and D. Hogan (eds), *The Law Society of Ireland, 1852–2002: portrait of a profession* (Dublin, 2002). A single eighteenth-century study is extant: C.E.B. Brett,

by Redmond) and the growth of the Law Society's library (dealt with by Byrne) are but two offerings in this invaluable book.

Hart's résumé of the order of serjeants in Ireland starts in the middle ages and ends with the last of the Irish serjeants in the twentieth century.[179] He had earlier dealt with the career of one seventeenth-century serjeant, Audley Mervyn.[180] Another lawyer from the same century, Patrick Darcy, prominent in the constitutional agitation of 1640 and 1641, is the subject of a separate study from O'Malley, while McGuire reassesses the career of Richard Nagle, James II's Irish attorney-general.[181] There is a seventeenth-century focus as well in Ohlmeyer's survey of recusant lawyers in the reign of Charles I – a survey that constitutes a continuation of research inspired by the late Donal Cregan.[182] Barnard, on the other hand, discusses the lawyers later in the same century.[183] Catholics and the profession are examined by both Kenny and Power.[184] Moving a good deal further on, Geoghegan has studied the involvement of the Bar in the events of 1798.[185]

In 1982, the Irish Manuscripts Commission published a list of all those admitted into membership of King's Inns between 1607 and 1867,[186] an indispensable work of reference for a period when attorneys

'Two eighteenth-century provincial attorneys: Matthew Brett and Jack Brett' in †Hogan and Osborough (eds), *Brehons*, as in fn. 177, p. 175.
179 †A.R. Hart, *A history of the king's serjeants at law in Ireland: honour rather than advantage?* (Dublin, 2000).
180 A.R. Hart, 'Audley Mervyn: lawyer or politician?', in †W.N. Osborough (ed.), *Explorations in law and history: Irish Legal History discourses, 1988–1994* (Dublin, 1995), p. 83.
181 L. O'Malley, 'Patrick Darcy – Galway lawyer and politician 1598–1668' in D. Ó Cearbhaill (ed.), *Galway, town and gown, 1484–1984* (Dublin, 1984), p. 90; J. McGuire, 'A lawyer in politics: the career of Sir Richard Nagle, c.1636–1699' in †Dawson (ed.), *Reflections*, as in fn. 27, p. 18 and in J. Devlin and H.B. Clarke (eds), *European encounters: essays in memory of Albert Lovett* (Dublin, 2003), p. 117.
182 J. Ohlmeyer, 'Irish recusant lawyers during the reign of Charles I' in M. Ó Siochrú (ed.), *Kingdoms in crisis: Ireland in the 1640s* (Dublin, 2001), p. 63. And see Donal F. Cregan, 'Irish Catholic admissions to the English inns of courts 1558–1603', *IJ*, 5 (1970), 95; idem, 'Irish recusant lawyers in politics in the reign of James I', *IJ*, 5 (1970), 306.
183 T.C. Barnard, 'Lawyers and the law in late seventeenth-century Ireland', *IHS*, 28 (1993), 256.
184 C. Kenny, 'The exclusion of Catholics from the legal profession in Ireland, 1537–1829', *IHS*, 25 (1987), 349; T. Power, 'Conversions among the legal profession in Ireland in the eighteenth century' in †Hogan and Osborough (eds), *Brehons*, as in fn. 177, p. 153.
185 P.M. Geoghegan, *1798 and the Irish Bar* (Dublin, 1998).
186 **King's Inns admission papers, 1607–1867*, ed. E. Keane, P. Beryl Eustace and Thomas

were obliged to be members as were barristers. A sequel, listing barristers only, from 1868 to the present day, was brought out in 2005.[187] This volume, edited by Ferguson, differs in a number of respects from the 1982 book. Attorneys (solicitors) are not included; much more biographical data is furnished; there are additional listings in a number of appendices; and there are illustrations (amongst which the photograph of the entire judicial bench for the superior courts in 1900 stands out). Ferguson himself contributes an essay on changes within the Irish barristers' profession for the years from the 1860s,[188] as does Osborough in a complementary contribution[189] – such matters as educational reform (1872); the abolition of the requirement to keep terms common in London (1885); the admission of women (1921); and the impact of Partition when Northern Ireland set up its own inn of court (1925). Ferguson's 'Portrait of the Irish Bar' supplies the names of 25 of its members who were killed in the First World War. These 25 are the subject of a separate study from Quinn.[190]

Philip Callan, a barrister and MP, was a prime mover in the campaign to end the requirement to keep terms common in London. Moran has furnished a biographical sketch.[191] Another prominent lawyer and politician, T.M. Healy, has had his career examined by Callanan.[192] Casey's *The Irish law officers* focuses primarily on the present day, but there is good historical coverage.[193] Edward Carson's successful advocacy in the Archer-Shee case – a case that inspired Rattigan's play *The Winslow Boy* – has been revisited by Lord Hutton.[194]

U. Sadlier (Dublin, 1982). The exercise was assisted by information contained in the Black Book of King's Inns, on which see T. Power, 'The Black Book of King's Inns: an introduction with an abstract of contents', *IJ*, 20 (1985), 135.
187 *King's Inns barristers, 1868–2004*, ed. K. Ferguson (Dublin, 2005).
188 'A portrait of the Irish bar, 1868–1968', ibid., pp 39–124.
189 'Landmarks in the history of King's Inns', ibid., pp 19–38.
190 †A.P. Quinn, *Wigs and guns: Irish barristers in the Great War* (Dublin, 2006).
191 G. Moran, 'Philip Callan: the rise and fall of an Irish nationalist MP, 1868–1885', *JLAS*, 22 (1992), 395.
192 F. Callanan, *T.M. Healy* (Cork, 1996); idem, 'T.M. Healy: the politics of advocacy' in †Dawson (ed.), *Reflections*, as in fn. 27, p. 51.
193 J. Casey, *The Irish law officers* (Dublin, 1996).
194 Lord Hutton, 'Sir Edward Carson KC and the Archer-Shee case' in †F.M. Larkin and N.M. Dawson (eds), *Lawyers, the law and history: Irish Legal History Society discourses and other papers, 2005–2009* (Dublin, forthcoming).

2.8 JUDICIAL BIOGRAPHY

The publication in 2004 of the 60 volumes of the *Oxford dictionary of national biography*, the successor to the old *DNB*, has provided the researcher with an invaluable, up-to-date work of reference. Many of the key actors in the history of law in Ireland have benefited from the reassessment that this major publishing initiative was to inspire. It would be otiose to furnish a list; the *Oxford DNB* is accessible on-line, and a quick search would show whether any Irish legal or judicial figure in whom the researcher might be interested is dealt with or not. Under way at present is a comparable project: a *Dictionary of Irish biography*. Publication is expected in 2008. Again, many individuals prominent in the history of law in Ireland are featured. (In fact, publication took place in 2009.)

One of the longer Irish legal entries in the *Oxford DNB* is Kavanaugh's account of John Fitzgibbon, the earl of Clare, successively attorney-general and lord chancellor, which is, in effect, a précis of her full-length biography of this central figure in Irish law and politics at the end of the eighteenth century.[195] Kavanaugh's assessments of the man merit being compared with those of Malcomson in the latter's lengthy introduction to a collection of Clare's letters and papers.[196] This important collection of documents sheds many a light on contemporary Irish politics as well as on Clare the man and the kind of work that engaged his attention in his successive official roles.

Two other collections of letters of Irish judicial personages have also been published. These are Hayton's edition of correspondence of Marmaduke Coghill, the early eighteenth-century judge of the Court of the Prerogative and Faculties,[197] and Kelly's edition of letters from Chief Baron Willes to the earl of Warwick in the middle of the same century.[198] Very different in style and content, both volumes again plug many gaps in our understanding of the legal system of the times and the political and social background against which it requires to be viewed. Coghill is to be counted among those members of the contemporary judiciary who also acted the part of entrepreneurs and

---

195 A.C. Kavanaugh, *John Fitzgibbon, earl of Clare: protestant reaction and English authority in late eighteenth-century Ireland* (Dublin, 1997).
196 **A volley of execrations: the letters and papers of John Fitzgibbon, earl of Clare, 1772–1802*, edited by D.A. Fleming and A.P.W. Malcomson (Dublin, 2005).
197 **Letters of Marmaduke Coghill, 1722–1738*, ed. D.W. Hayton (Dublin, 2005).
198 *The letters of Lord Chief Baron Edward Willes to the earl of Warwick, 1757–62: an account of Ireland in the mid-eighteenth century*, ed. J. Kelly (Aberystwyth, 1990).

improving landlords, a role filled by them which is examined by Osborough.[199]

O'Carroll's book on Robert Day, a puisne judge in King's Bench, straddles the eighteenth and nineteenth centuries.[200] Based largely on Day's own diaries and on his addresses to grand juries, the book is a nice companion volume to a biography of Day published in the 1930s.[201] Rather more of Day's grand jury addresses are extant – in the library of the Royal Irish Academy – than O'Carroll has felt able to reproduce. On these addresses generally, it is to be noted that a small selection is printed in a contribution for the Camden Society that contains such addresses for both England and Ireland.[202] Here Ireland is represented by addresses from Thomas Marlay (1749), Richard Aston (1763), and Denis George (1798), as well as by two from Day (1793 and 1796).

Biographical material on the Irish judges has appeared at infrequent intervals in a variety of publications. Costello tackles the short career as judge of the Irish Admiralty in the seventeenth century of Sir William Petty.[203] Daire Hogan discusses the extraordinary sequence of judicial appointments in the 1860s in one article; the conflict between Jonathan Christian and Thomas O'Hagan in the Court of Appeal in Chancery in a second, and the career of Lord Chief Justice Cherry, 1914–16, in a third.[204] Kenny deals with the career of Lord Plunket, especially during the years 1827 to 1841;[205] and the late Lord Lowry, himself a lord of appeal in ordinary, proffers a fresh view on all the preceding Irish appointments to the House of Lords – Fitzgerald, Morris, Atkinson, Macnaghten, Russell, Carson, and MacDermott –

199 W.N. Osborough, 'Extramural pursuits of the eighteenth-century bench' in Breen, Casey and Kerr (eds), *Liber memorialis*, as in fn. 92, p. 317.
200 G. O'Carroll, *Robert Day (1746–1841): the diaries and addresses to the grand juries, 1793–1829* (Tralee, Co. Kerry, 2004).
201 E.B. Day, *Mr Justice Day of Kerry: a discursive memoir* (Exeter, 1938).
202 'Charges to the grand jury', ed. G. Lamoine, *Camden Society, 4th series*, 43 (London, 1992).
203 K. Costello, 'Sir William Petty and the court of Admiralty in Restoration Ireland' in †Brand, Costello and Osborough (eds), *Adventures*, as in fn. 66, p. 106.
204 D. Hogan, 'Vacancies for their friends: judicial appointments in 1866–1867' in †Hogan and Osborough (eds), *Brehons*, as in fn. 177, p. 211; 'Arrows too sharply pointed: the relations of Lord Justice Christian and Lord O'Hagan' in McEldowney and O'Higgins (eds), *The common law*, as in fn. 112, p. 61; 'R.R. Cherry, lord chief justice of Ireland 1914–1916' in †Greer and Dawson (eds), *Mysteries*, as in fn. 22, p. 161.
205 C. Kenny, 'Irish ambition and English preference in chancery appointments, 1827–1841: the fate of William Conyngham Plunket' in Osborough (ed.), *Explorations*, as in fn. 180, p. 133.

in a piece which reproduces portraits of each one of them.[206] Larkin prints a letter on the events of 1916 written by a county court judge at the time, Judge Bodkin.[207] Osborough's essay on the campaign by Sir Thomas Molony, the last lord chief justice, to retain his title has been reprinted.[208] Ó Broin, for his part, has focused on one aspect of the extraordinary career of W.E. Wylie.[209]

Four resident magistrates – J.C. Milling, J.W. Flanagan, E.J.C. Dease and W.J. O'Reilly (two of whom – Milling and Flanagan – were assassinated) – have their careers related by Bonsall in her book on the RMs.[210] Molony's effective successor, the first chief justice of the Irish Free State, Hugh Kennedy, left a wealth of papers at his death in 1936. Holland has produced a guide to these,[211] whilst Gerard Hogan has dealt in detail with one curious case that it fell to Kennedy to decide in his judicial capacity: the application of a judge under the former British dispensation to be admitted to the roll of solicitors.[212] One subsequent chief justice in the South has penned an autobiography.[213]

For Northern Ireland, a biography of its first lord chief justice, Sir Denis Henry, has come from McDonnell.[214] A distinguished later occupant of the position, Lord MacDermott, who, as we have seen, also served on the House of Lords, left an impressive autobiographical fragment.[215] Another judicial memoir from Northern Ireland was produced by Lord Justice Jones.[216]

---

206 Lord Lowry, 'The Irish lords of appeal in ordinary' in †Greer and Dawson (eds), *Mysteries*, as in fn. 22, p. 193.
207 F.M. Larkin, 'Judge Bodkin and the 1916 Rising: a letter to his son' in †Dawson (ed.), *Reflections*, as in fn. 27, p. 67.
208 'The title of the last lord chief justice of Ireland', reprinted in Osborough, *Studies*, as in fn. 7, p. 315.
209 L. Ó Broin, *W.E. Wylie and the Irish revolution, 1916–1921* (Dublin, 1989).
210 P. Bonsall, *The Irish RMs: the resident magistrates in the British administration of Ireland* (Dublin, n.d. [1997]).
211 A.C. Holland, 'The papers of Hugh Kennedy: a research legacy for the foundation of the State', *IJ*, 24 (1989), 279.
212 G.W. Hogan, 'Chief Justice Kennedy and Sir James O'Connor's application', *IJ*, 23 (1988), 144.
213 T.F. O'Higgins, *A double life* (Dublin, 1996).
214 A.D. McDonnell, *The life of Sir Denis Henry Catholic Unionist* (Belfast, 2000).
215 J.C. MacDermott, *An enriching life* (1980).
216 E. Jones, *His life and times: the autobiography of the rt. hon. Sir Edward Jones* (Enniskillen, Co. Fermanagh, 1987).

2.9 COURTHOUSES

A volume published under the auspices of the Irish Heritage Council supplies a photographic record for courthouses in the Republic.[217] Accompanying text concentrates on architectural detail. An introductory essay by Niall McCullough offers an historical perspective but suffers from being much too brief. Brett's volume dealing, inter alia, with courthouses in Ulster and brought out by the Ulster Architectural Heritage Society is superior in its conception.[218] A comprehensive history for the courthouses in the entire island is sorely needed.

Faltering steps in the right direction will be found in a number of essays brought together by Caroline Costello to mark the bicentenary of Gandon's Four Courts building in Dublin.[219] The reader is likely to find of enduring interest in this collection Kenny's contribution on the history of the site itself,[220] two contributions from McParland on the old site of the Four Courts and on the early years at the new site, two contributions from Curran, especially the one on 'Figures in the Hall', Keane's piece on the destruction of June 1922, and Gerard Hogan's on the eventual return to the restored building in 1931.

2.10 LEGAL WRITING AND PUBLISHING

Much attention has in recent years been devoted to what hitherto had been a somewhat neglected topic: the history of Irish legal writing and publishing. In the main, this has been due to the holding of a series of lectures on Irish legal bibliography organized by Hugh Fitzpatrick, a Dublin solicitor. Osborough's tendentiously entitled lecture, with its reference to a challenge as yet unmet, argued that a large amount of original research remained a prerequisite.[221] O'Higgins, the doyen of Irish legal bibliography studies and the author of a classic work of reference,[222] has given us his thoughts on 'puzzles' in the area.[223] Greer

---

217 M. Dunne and B. Philips, compilers, *The courthouses of Ireland: a gazetteer of Irish courthouses* (Kilkenny, 1999). Despite the title, this book only deals with the courthouses in the 26 counties of the Republic.
218 C.E.B. Brett, *Courthouses and market-houses of the province of Ulster* (Belfast, 1973).
219 Costello (ed.), *Four Courts*, as in fn. 12.
220 See, too, Kenny's 'The Four Courts in Dublin before 1796', *IJ*, 21 (1986), 107.
221 W.N. Osborough, 'The history of Irish legal publishing: a challenge unmet', *IJ*, 35 (2000), 355.
222 P. O'Higgins, *A bibliography of Irish trials and other legal proceedings* (Abingdon, Oxon, 1986).
223 P. O'Higgins, 'An essay on puzzles in Irish legal bibliography', *IJ*, 36 (2001), 214.

pronounced on one specific genre of texts – those dealing with criminal justice.[224] McEldowney focused on the role of biography in legal history,[225] while Cohen concentrated on the link between Ireland and early American legal literature.[226] Aside from all the Fitzpatrick lectures, Sweeney has examined the contribution to admiralty law of the late eighteenth-century Irish civilian, Arthur Browne,[227] and Kenny has detailed the career of Bartholomew Duhigg, the first historian of King's Inns,[228] whilst Osborough has surveyed the career and publications of John Finlay, a prolific early nineteenth-century legal author.[229] Osborough has also dealt with the financial and other problems that faced the Irish King's printer, George Grierson II, following adoption of the Act of Union in 1800 and the circumstance that there were thenceforward no statutes of an Irish parliament to print.[230] Elsewhere the same author has dealt with the history of Irish law reporting and the story of the statute-book of the pre-Union Irish parliament.[231]

The late twentieth-century boom in Irish legal publishing is the focus of Buckley's contribution to the collection of essays edited by Hall and Daire Hogan.[232] Buckley helpfully lists books published by the Law Society of Ireland and those assisted by the Arthur Cox Foundation. A few of the volumes in both categories deal with facets of Irish legal history.

---

224 D. Greer, 'Crime, justice and legal literature in nineteenth-century Ireland', *IJ*, 37 (2002), 241.
225 J. McEldowney, 'Challenges in legal bibliography: the role of biography in legal history', *IJ*, 39 (2004), 215. See, too, his 'Dicey and the sovereignty of parliament: lessons from Irish legal history' in †Dawson (ed.), *Reflections*, as in fn. 27, p. 32.
226 M.L. Cohen, 'Irish influences on early American law books: authors, printers and subjects', *IJ*, 36 (2001), 199.
227 J.C. Sweeney, 'Admiralty law of Arthur Browne', *Journal of Maritime Law and Commerce*, 26 (1995), 59.
228 C. Kenny, 'Counsellor Duhigg: antiquarian and activist', *IJ*, 21 (1986), 300.
229 W.N. Osborough, 'Publishing the law: John Finlay (1780–1856)' in M. Fanning and R. Gillespie (eds), *Print culture and intellectual life in Ireland, 1660–1941: essays in honour of Michael Adams* (Dublin, 2006), p. 53.
230 W.N. Osborough, 'Tribulations of a king's printer: George Grierson II in court' in C. Benson and S. Fitzpatrick (eds), *That woman! Studies in Irish bibliography: a festschrift for Mary Paul Pollard* (Dublin, 2005), 28.
231 'Puzzles from Irish law reporting history' in P. Birks (ed.), *The life of the law: proceedings of the 10th British Legal History Conference, Oxford, 1991* (London, Rio Grande, 1993), p. 89; 'The legislation of the pre-Union Irish parliament', introduction to the 1995 reprint of the Irish Statutes revised edition (see fn. 236, below), p. A. Both these pieces are reprinted in Osborough, *Studies*, as in fn. 7.
232 J.F. Buckley, 'Legal publishing' in Hall and Hogan (eds), *Law Society*, as in fn. 178, p. 189.

64   An island's law

There have been a few new editions of older classic texts. Caldicott, as already noted, has edited Patrick Darcy's *An argument* of 1643 for the Camden Society series,[233] and Donlan has brought out a fresh edition of F.S. Sullivan's lectures originally published in 1776.[234] In addition, it is worth recognition that a translation into French of William Molyneux's *The case of Ireland*, first published in Dublin in 1698, has appeared from the Presses Universitaires de Caen.[235] Reprints deserve a mention too. *The Irish Statutes revised edition of 1885* was reissued in 1995[236] and the *Irish Parliamentary Register* covering the years from 1781 to 1797 in 1999.[237] A single volume emanating from the project to recalendar the Tudor State Papers relating to Ireland made a welcome appearance in 2000.[238]

2.11 CONCLUSION

Despite the huge amount of research, writing and publication that has occurred in the last twenty years or so, there remain considerable gaps in our understanding of the history of law in Ireland. A number of these gaps it would be possible to fill were a sufficient number of individuals in the years ahead attracted to this field of intellectual labour. A particular challenge thus faces both the Irish historian and the Irish lawyer.[239] Legal aspects to the development of the Irish capital

---

233 'Patrick Darcy, an Argument', ed. C.E.J. Caldicott, *Camden Miscellany*, 31 (*Camden Society, 4th series*, 44) (London, 1992), 191.
234 F.S. Sullivan, *Lectures on the constitution and laws of England with a commentary on Magna Carta, etc.*, ed. S.P. Donlan (Clark, NJ, 2003).
235 *Discours sur la sujétion de l'Irlande*, trans. J. Genet and E. Hellegouarc'h with introduction by P. Gouhier (Caen, 1995).
236 *The Irish Statutes revised edition: 3 Edward II to the Union, A.D. 1310–1800* (Dublin, 1885), repr. (Dublin, 1995).
237 *The Parliamentary Register of Ireland, 1781–1797*, 17 vols, with new introduction by W.J. McCormack (Bristol and Tokyo, 1999). See, too, A.P.W. Malcomson and D.J. Jackson, 'Sir Henry Cavendish and proceedings of the Irish House of Commons, 1776–1800' in Hayton (ed.), *Irish parliament*, as in fn. 27, p. 128.
238 **Calendar of State Papers, Ireland: Tudor period, 1571–1575*, ed. M. O'Dowd (London and Dublin, 2000). The final volume in the Early Irish Statutes series, it should be noted, has also appeared: *Statute rolls of the Irish parliament, Richard III–Henry VIII*, edited by P. Connolly (Dublin, 2002).
239 See further W.N. Osborough, 'Mysteries and solutions: experiencing Irish legal history' in †Greer and Dawson (eds), *Mysteries*, as in fn. 22, p. 217; idem, 'Bishop Dixon, the Irish historian and Irish law', *NILQ*, 59 (2006), 1.

Dublin represents one attempt to popularize this field of study,[240] Hickey's book on popular attitudes to be derived from modern folk tradition another.[241] Further such efforts are called for.

2.12 ADDENDA

Four volumes that have appeared since this bibliographical essay was originally prepared are important and merit mention. Two cover key episodes in seventeenth-century Irish history and print a wealth of archival material: both hail from the Irish Manuscripts Commission.[242] The operation of Poynings' Law in the period from the Restoration down to the Act of Union is the focus of a magisterial study from Kelly.[243] And, finally, Hall has pieced together the story of law reporting in Ireland.[244]

---

240 †W.N. Osborough, *Law and the emergence of modern Dublin: a litigation topography for a capital city* (Dublin, 1996).
241 †E. Hickey, *Irish law and lawyers in modern folk tradition* (Dublin, 1999).
242 **The Irish Commission of 1622: an investigation of the Irish Administration, 1615–1622, and its consequences*, ed. V. Treadwell (Dublin, 2006); **Court of Claims: submissions and evidence, 1663*, ed. G. Tallon (Dublin, 2006).
243 †J. Kelly, *Poynings' Law and the making of law in Ireland, 1660–1800* (Dublin, 2007).
244 E.G. Hall, *The Superior Courts of law: official law reporting in Ireland, 1866–2006* (Dublin, 2007).

Further writing on Irish legal history (2012)

3.1 EARLY IRISH LAW

The major event in the last twenty odd years was to be the publication by Kelly from the School of Celtic Studies at the Dublin Institute for Advanced Studies of his long-awaited *Guide* to the entire subject.[1] This was then followed by the same author's work on early Irish farming, an exercise inspired by the wealth of information on that topic to be found in the law tracts themselves.[2] Another essential tool of reference was set to emerge from the same stable in 2005, Breatnach's *Companion* to Binchy's magisterial *Corpus Iuris Hibernici*.[3] Ó Cathasaigh, heralding this last as 'a magnificent achievement', explained why the *Companion* was sorely needed. The *Corpus* possessed no table of contents, and the reader opening it at random had nothing to tell him what text it was or what kind of text.[4]

In addition, a major overview of the challenge involved in studying early Irish law has come from the pen of Charles-Edwards in volume 1 of the *New history*.[5] There are excellent insights too in the chapters touching on law in a general history of early medieval Ireland from Ó Cróinín.[6] Of free-standing monographs that have also appeared particular mention needs to be made of McLeod on contract law[7] and of Stacey on developments from suretyship to a world of courts and

---

1 Fergus Kelly, *A guide to early Irish law* (Dublin, 1988).
2 Fergus Kelly, *Early Irish farming* (Dublin, 1995).
3 Liam Breatnach, *A companion to the Corpus Iuris Hibernici* (Dublin, 2005). Note this volume's cover: a colour photograph of the site of the medieval law school of the O'Davorens at Cahermacnaghten in the Burren of Co. Clare.
4 Tomas Ó Cathasaigh, reviewing the *Companion* in *Stud Hib*, 34 (2006–7), 193.
5 T.M. Charles-Edwards, 'Early Irish law' in *A new history of Ireland: i – prehistoric and early Ireland*, ed. Dáibhí Ó Cróinín (Oxford, 2005), p. 331.
6 Dáibhí Ó Cróinín, *Early medieval Ireland, 400–1200* (London, 1995), chs. 3, 4 and 5.
7 Neil McLeod, *Early Irish contract law* (Sydney, n.d., 1992).

rulers (including Welsh material).[8] Of outstanding interest on the later history of the brehon law are two provocative papers from Patterson.[9] Perceptions and interpretation of early Irish law in even later centuries – the nineteenth and the twentieth – are tackled in original essays from Mohr.[10]

Exhaustive bibliographies for the entire subject will be found in Kelly's *Guide*, vol. 1 of the *New history*, Stacey's *Road to judgment* and Ó Cróinín's *Early medieval Ireland*. It seems right even so in this short survey to draw attention to publications concentrating on editions of primary texts, of which there have been several. Such publications have come from Breatnach,[11] Carey,[12] Kelly,[13] Ní Dhonnchadha[14] and Poppe.[15]

In addition, important individual essays are to be found in a number of composite works, such as the collection edited by McCone and Simms on *Progress in medieval Irish studies*,[16] that by Ó Corráin, Breatnach and McCone in honour of Professor James Carney,[17] that by Davies and Fouracre on *The settlement of disputes*,[18] and that by Ní Chatháin and Richter on *Ireland and Christendom*.[19]

---

8 R.C. Stacey, *The road to judgment: from custom to court in medieval Ireland and Wales* (Philadelphia, 1994).

9 N.T. Patterson, 'Brehon law in the late middle ages: "antiquarian and obsolete" or "traditional and functional"?' *Cambridge Medieval Celtic Studies*, 17 (1989), 43; 'Gaelic law and the Tudor conquest of Ireland: the social background of the sixteenth-century recensions of the pseudo-historical prologue to the Senchas Már', *IHS*, 27 (1991), 193.

10 Thomas Mohr, 'Law in a Gaelic Utopia: perceptions of brehon law in nineteenth- and early twentieth-century Ireland' in O. Brupbacher et al. (eds), *Remembering and forgetting: yearbook of legal history* (Munich, 2007), p. 247; 'Brehon law before twentieth century courts', *Peritia*, 16 (2002), 352.

11 Liam Breatnach, *Uraicecht na Ríar: the poetic grades in early Irish law* (Dublin, 1987); 'The first third of Bretha Nemed Toísech', *Ériu*, 40 (1989), 1.

12 John Carey, 'An edition of the pseudo-historical prologue to the Senchas Már', *Eriu*, 45 (1994), 1.

13 Fergus Kelly, *Audacht Moraind* (Dublin, 1976); 'An Old-Irish text on court procedure', *Peritia*, 5 (1986), 74.

14 Máirín Ní Dhonnchadha, 'The Lex innocentium: Adomnan's law for women, clerics and youths, 697 A.D.' in Mary O'Dowd and Sabine Wichert (eds), *Chattel, servant or citizen: women's status in church, state and society* (Hist. Studies, XIX; Belfast, 1995), p. 58.

15 Erich Poppe, 'A new edition of Cáin Éimíne Báin', *Celtica*, 18 (1986), 35; 'The genealogy of Émin(e) in the Book of Leinster', *Ériu*, 40 (1989), 93.

16 Kim McCone and Katharine Simms (eds), *Progress in medieval Irish studies* (Maynooth, 1996).

17 Donnchadh Ó Corráin, Liam Breatnach and Kim McCone (eds), *Sages, saints and storytellers: Celtic studies in honour of Professor James Carney* (Maynooth, 1989).

18 W. Davies and P. Fouracre (eds), *The settlement of disputes in early medieval Europe* (Cambridge, 1986).

19 Próinséas Ní Chatháin and Michael Richter (eds), *Irland und die Christenheit:*

Among the wealth of recent secondary works, the following may be highlighted:

(i) Breatnach on lawyers, the law and on the original extent of the Senchas Már;[20]
(ii) Carey on facets of Dubthach's judgment, and on evidence from the dead;[21]
(iii) Clancy on the Irish penitentials,[22] a topic touched on as well by Gerriets;[23]
(iv) Charles-Edwards, who besides writing on the Irish canons,[24] a topic of interest to Price,[25] deals with the pastoral role of the church, compares Irish and Welsh kinship, and examines evidence for any sort of *contrat social* in the political arrangements;
(v) Henry on procedure and status;[26]
(vi) Jaski on marriage laws;[27]
(vii) Mori on monks and inheritance laws;[28]
(viii) Ó Corráin on fences and fencing;[29]

Bibelstudien und Mission/Ireland and Christendom: the Bible and the missions (Stuttgart, 1987).
20 Liam Breatnach, 'Lawyers in early Ireland' in †D. Hogan and W.N. Osborough (eds), *Brehons, serjeants and attorneys: studies in the history of the Irish legal profession* (Dublin, 1990); 'Law' in Kim McCone and Katharine Simms (eds), *Progress in medieval Irish studies* (Maynooth, 1996), p. 107; 'On the original extent of the Senchas Már', *Ériu*, 47 (1996), 1.
21 John Carey, 'The two laws in Dubthach's judgment', *Cambridge Medieval Celtic Studies*, 19 (1990), 1; 'The testimony of the dead', *Éigse*, 26 (1992), 1.
22 F.G. Clancy, 'The Irish penitentials', *Milltown Studies*, 21(1988), 87.
23 Marilyn Gerriets, 'Theft, penitentials and the compilation of the early Irish laws', *Celtica*, 22 (1991), 18.
24 T.M. Charles-Edwards, 'The construction of the Hibernensis', *Peritia*, 12 (1998), 209; 'The pastoral role of the church in the early Irish laws' in John Blair and Richard Sharpe (eds), *Pastoral care before the parish* (Leicester, 1992); *Early Irish and Welsh kinship* (Oxford, 1993); 'A contract between king and people in early medieval Ireland? Crith Gablach on kingship', *Peritia*, 8 (1994), 107.
25 Huw Price, 'Early Irish canons and medieval Welsh law', *Peritia*, 5 (1986), 107.
26 P.L. Henry, 'A note on the Brehon law tracts of procedure and status, Coíc Conara Fugill and Uraicecht Becc', *ZCP*, 49–50 (1997), 311.
27 Bart Jaski, 'Marriage laws in Ireland and on the Continent in the early middle ages' in C.E. Meek and M.K. Simms (eds), *The fragility of her sex? Medieval Irish women in their European context* (Dublin, 1996), p. 16.
28 Setsuko Mori, 'Irish monasticism and the concept of inheritance: an examination of its legal aspects' in Taro Matsuo (ed.), *Comparative aspects of Irish and Japanese economic and social history* (Tokyo, 1993), p. 123.
29 Donnchadh Ó Corráin, 'Some legal references to fences and fencing in early historic Ireland' in Terence Reeves-Smyth and Fred Hammond (eds), *Landscape archaeology in Ireland* (Oxford, 1983), p. 247.

(ix) Patterson on kinship law;[30] and
(x) Stacey on immunities.[31]

3.2 MEDIEVAL IRELAND

Veach has engaged in a reassessment of Henry II's grant of Meath to de Lacy in the 1170s,[32] whilst Phillips has examined the role of Archbishop MacCarwell of Cashel at the end of the thirteenth century in the attempted purchase of the English common law for the Irish.[33]

A major record source for medieval financial transactions – that for Irish Exchequer payments – has been edited by the late Philomena Connolly.[34] Corruption in the Irish Exchequer itself in 1421 leading to Lord Slane's holding of the manor of Slane being entered up in the White Book of the Exchequer as held directly of the King (and rendering him liable, accordingly, for payments of scutage) is the subject of a fascinating piece of detective work from Mercer.[35] This affair and the dispute at the end of the thirteenth century over the Comyn inheritance (were the lands held by knight service or socage?)[36] raises the perhaps insoluble problem of the frequency of these conflicts over tenurial status under the feudal legal order in medieval Ireland.

Another Armagh register – that of Nicholas Fleming – has been brought out under the aegis of the Irish Manuscripts Commission.

It will not be inappropriate to append here a list of the volumes to have appeared so far:

---

30 N.T. Patterson, *Early Irish kinship: the legal structure of the agnatic descent group* (Boston, 1988); 'Patrilineal groups in early Irish society: the evidence from the Irish law texts', *Bulletin of the Board of Celtic Studies*, 37 (1990), 133.
31 R.C. Stacey, 'Ties that bind: immunities in Celtic law', *Cambridge Medieval Celtic Studies*, 20 (1990), p. 39. See, too, Stacey's translation of Berrad Airechta in T.M. Charles-Edwards, Morfydd E. Owen and D.B. Walters (eds), *Lawyers and lawmen: studies in the history of law presented to Professor Dafydd Jenkins on his 75th birthday* (Cardiff, 1986), p. 210.
32 Colm T. Veach, 'Henry II's grant of Meath to Hugh de Lacy in 1172', *Ríocht na Midhe*, 18 (2007), 17.
33 Seymour Phillips, 'David MacCarwell and the proposal to purchase English law, *c*.1273–*c*.1280', *Peritia*, 10 (1996), 253.
34 **Irish Exchequer payments, 1270–1446*, ed. Philomena Connolly (Dublin, IMC, 1998).
35 Malcolm Mercer, 'Select document: Exchequer malpractice in late medieval Ireland: a petition from Christopher Fleming, Lord Slane, 1438', *IHS*, 36 (2009), 407.
36 G.J. Hand, 'The common law in Ireland in the 13th and 14th centuries: two cases involving Christ Church, Dublin', *JRSAI*, 97 (1967), 97.

(i) *The register of John Swayne, archbishop of Armagh, 1418–1439*, ed. D.A. Chart (Belfast: HMSO; 1935);
(ii) *Registrum Iohannis Mey: the register of John Mey, archbishop of Armagh, 1443–1456*, ed. W.G.H. Quigley and E.F.D. Roberts (Belfast: HMSO; 1972);
(iii) **The register of Milo Sweteman, archbishop of Armagh, 1361–1380*, ed. Brendan Smith (Dublin, IMC; 1996);
(iv) **Registrum Octaviani: the register of Octavian de Palatio, archbishop of Armagh, 1478–1513*, ed. M. Sughi, 2 vols (Dublin, IMC; 1999); and
(v) **The register of Nicholas Fleming, archbishop of Armagh, 1404–1416*, ed. Brendan Smith (Dublin, IMC; 2003).

Still outstanding are modern editions for the registers of two other archbishops of Armagh: John Prene, 1439–43 and George Cromer, 1521–43.

One further milestone of which note assuredly must also be taken has been the publication in three volumes, courtesy of the Church of England Record Society, of records of Irish convocations from 1101 down to 1869.[37]

3.3 THE POST-MEDIEVAL LEGAL SYSTEM IN THE COMMON LAW DISPENSATION

For the Tudor period note might first be taken of the appearance of a second volume in the major project for the revised edition of the State Papers for Ireland, 1509–1585. The first volume to appear covered the years 1571 to 1575; this new volume, edited by Cunningham, is confined to the years 1566 and 1567.[38]

At this time the Ormond palatinate or liberty of Tipperary continued to embody a distinct jurisdictional entity. Denied the authority to deal with the traditional pleas of the crown, the earls of Ormond yet possessed very considerable other powers – the promulgation of ordinances to govern the territory, for instance. A number of these 'ordinances' stretching from 1564 to 1608 are now introduced in a

---

37 *Records of Convocation: xvi Ireland, 1101–1690; xvii Ireland 1690–1869 (Part 1): xviii Ireland 1690–1869 (Part 2)*. All ed. Gerald Bray (Woodbridge, Suffolk; 2006).
38 **Calendar of State Papers Ireland, Tudor period 1566–1567, revised edition*, ed. Bernadette Cunningham (Dublin, IMC, 2009).

major break-through piece of research from Edwards and Empey.[39] One of the 1564 documents, conveniently reproduced, is styled 'Orders to be kept in the contre of Typerary'; that of 1608 'statutes enacted in the court of the liberty of Tipperary'.

Much less is known of the Desmond palatinate of Kerry which ended with the attainder of the 15th earl in 1582. A new study from McCormack of the earldom of Desmond itself for the last 120 years of its existence does, however, illuminate a few dark corners.[40] The failure in 1613, a few years later, by Thomas Lutterell of Lutterellston to complete the oath of supremacy has inspired Ní Mhurchadha to revisit the difficult topic of oaths in Irish history and the consequences of failure properly to subscribe them.[41]

Overlapping with Desmond, there was to be established in 1570 the presidency of Munster, which lasted until 1672. In the early 1600s the president of Munster was Sir Henry Brouncker, who was none too pleased when a military man who had received from him a commission of martial law was put on trial at the Limerick assizes in 1606 for abusing his powers. He had summarily arrested and sanctioned the hanging of two jesters, in Clonshire, Co. Limerick, a misdeed which alarmed sundry royal officials, leading to the man in question, one John Downing, being indicted for murder. The trial was to be aborted when Brouncker, one of the judges, stormed out after the jury returned a guilty verdict. Downing who carried unsavoury baggage – complicity in the mass execution of rebel prisoners on Dursey Island off the coast of Co. Cork in 1602 – was never in fact to be sentenced, and was later pardoned. The whole extraordinary tale has now been related by Edwards who manages in the process to shed light on a number of topics – martial law commissions, the vagrancy laws, the empanelling of juries, and the relationship of the assizes to presidency jurisdiction.[42]

Like its counterpart for Connaught, the Munster presidency was modelled on the better-known provincial administrative set-up, again of Tudor inspiration, for England, such as the Council of the North

39 David Edwards and Adrian Empey, 'Tipperary liberty ordinances of the "black" earl of Ormond' in David Edwards (ed.), *Regions and rulers in Ireland, 1100–1650: essays for Kenneth Nicholls* (Dublin, 2004), p. 122.
40 A.M. McCormack, *The earldom of Desmond, 1463–1583: the decline and crisis of a feudal lordship* (Dublin, 2005).
41 Maighréad Ní Mhurchadha, 'Documents concerning the oath of supremacy in early seventeenth-century Ireland', *Anal Hib*, 67 (2010), 264.
42 David Edwards, 'Two fools and a martial law commissioner: cultural conflict at the Limerick assizes of 1606' in idem (ed.), *Regions and rulers in Ireland*, p. 237.

and the Council of the Marches of Wales. One record of the Munster presidency's proceedings, covering a half century, came into the possession of Bishop Stillingfleet, bishop of Worcester, and whilst most of Stillingfleet's library, on his death, was acquired by Archbishop Narcissus Marsh for the library in Dublin still in existence which bears Marsh's name, this invaluable manuscript record was purchased by Robert Harley for the princely sum of £2 3s., and came to be known as Harleian MS 697. It has now, finally, been transcribed and published under the aegis of the Irish Manuscripts Commission.[43] The index to the subject-matter illustrates the extraordinary variety of matters dealt with by the presidency's council. Tithes and ale-houses and much else merited attention, and there are entries too for provincial court cases (in English) and records of assizes and gaol deliveries (in Latin) as well. The appearance of what is the sole surviving council book for either of the two Irish presidencies marks a major achievement, throwing considerable light, as it does, on the pattern of the entire legal system in the devolved, if short-lived, provincial regime.

A very different lacuna in the historiography – the treatment of the Irish language in the eighteenth and early nineteenth centuries – has been filled by Ní Mhunghaile.[44] Another lacuna of a very different kind, touching on the conflict between a manager of Dublin's Crow Street Theatre and a newspaper editor and covering a range of topics, has been filled in a study from Greene that is blessed with a title one of the longest to greet the reader of Ireland's mainstream history periodicals.[45]

From Greene's survey one topic in particular is worth pointing out – the controversy that erupted in 1789 and 1790 over the employment by the court of King's Bench of the judicially sanctioned *fiat* in defamation suits. Greene's coverage of the many different issues that separated John Magee, the newspaper editor, from Richard Daly, the theatre manager, and his other adversaries, sheds a great deal of light on the row over the earl of Clonmell's endorsement of the *fiat*, which supplements what we have of the House of Commons debate of

---

43 *The Council Book for the province of Munster, c.1599–1649*, ed. M.C. Clayton (Dublin, IMC; 2008).

44 Lesa Ní Mhunghaile, 'The legal system in Ireland and the Irish language, 1700–c.1843' in Michael Brown and S.P. Donlan (eds), *The law and other legalities of Ireland, 1689–1850* (Farnham, Surrey, 2011), p. 325.

45 J.C. Greene, 'The trials of Richard Daly and John Magee, involving the Sham Squire, the Lottery Swindle of 1788, the Billiard Marker's Ghost, and the Grand Olympic pig hunt', *Eighteenth-Century Ireland*, 24 (2009), 135.

3 March 1790 on that very topic.[46] This was the occasion when the Commons voted 125–91 in support of Ponsonby's resolution that:

> The issuing of writs from courts of justice in actions of suits for defamation, where the sum of damages could not be fairly ascertained and the holding persons on special bail in excessive sums thereon, is illegal, and subversive of the liberty of the subject.

The jury system in the eighteenth century and in the earlier nineteenth has been explored in two complementary offerings by Howlin, the first concentrating on special juries in Dublin, and the second on differences in the laws regulating juries as between Ireland and England.[47] There is much more on the nineteenth-century jury in Vaughan's magisterial volume on murder trials, of which detailed note is taken below. And facets of the office of sheriff, including sales authorized by him, were to be explored by Pole.[48]

Not easy to classify, but since part of the story of any legal system is the impact it can have on the intelligence of the observer or bystander, it is best entered up here – Mr Justice Hardiman's survey devoted to James Joyce and the law.[49]

Mary Kotsonouris' two books on the Dáil Courts and on their winding-up focused on the wholly exceptional character facing a legal system during a period of revolutionary turmoil.[50] The same period has captured the attention of David Foxton,[51] but from a somewhat different perspective. His *Revolutionary lawyers* examines the paradoxes of the struggle for Irish independence where Sinn Féin would at the same

---

46 *Parl. reg. Ire*, X, 358 (3 March 1790).
47 Niamh Howlin, 'Merchants and esquires: special juries in Dublin, 1725–1833' in Gillian O'Brien and Finola O'Kane (eds), *Georgian Dublin* (Dublin, 2008), p. 97; eadem, 'English and Irish jury laws: the growing divergence, 1825–1833' in Brown & Donlan (eds), *Law and other legalities of Ireland*, p. 117. See, too, her 'Controlling jury composition in nineteenth-century Ireland', *Journal of Legal History*, 30 (2009), 227.
48 †Adam Pole, 'Role of the sheriff in Victorian Ireland' in F.M. Larkin and N.M. Dawson (eds), *Lawyers, the law and history: Irish Legal History Society discourses and other papers, 2005–2011* (Dublin, forthcoming); idem, 'Sheriffs' sales during the land war, 1879–82', *IHS*, 34 (2005), 386.
49 †Adrian Hardiman, 'Law, crime and punishment in Bloomsday Dublin' in Larkin & Dawson (eds), *Lawyers, the law and history* (forthcoming).
50 Mary Kotsonouris, *Retreat from revolution: the Dáil courts, 1920–24* (Dublin, 1994); eadem, †*The winding-up of the Dáil courts, 1922–1925: an obvious duty* (Dublin, 2004).
51 David Foxton, *Revolutionary lawyers: Sinn Féin and Crown Courts in Ireland and Britain, 1916–1923* (Dublin, 2008).

time deny the authority of the Crown Courts yet simultaneously employ the rule of law to further their cause.

3.4 CONSTITUTIONAL LAW

The restructuring of the Irish administration under the Tudors had many facets. One was the establishment half way through the reign of Elizabeth I of the office of secretary of state for Ireland, a departure which has now been analysed by Barry.[52] Commissions of martial law made their appearance as well, their functioning under James I and VI having been scrutinized by Edwards.[53]

In the seventeenth century constitutional discourse came to be focused on the key questions of Irish legislative competence and Irish legislative independence. William Molyneux's *The case of Ireland's ... stated* of 1689 was early into print and is well known. Two other enterprises of a similar tendency, one attributed to Sir Richard Bolton, an Irish lord chancellor, and the other to Sir William Domville, the Restoration attorney general, have now at last been introduced to the public at large by Kelly.[54] The second of the salient articles by Kelly helpfully compares and contrasts the approaches of the three authors. There is an impressive opening paragraph in Domville's 'Disquisition', which merits quotation. 'In handling of this Question', he writes,

> I conceive it necessary first to Consult the Historians and Writers of Elder Times, and then with the Resolutions and Authorytys of those who have lately written of the Municipall Lawes of both Kingdomes: for as this latter affords us Variety of Opinions, so the former Will Yeild us much Light to Discover the Truth, [and]

---

52 Judith Barry, 'Sir Geoffrey Fenton and the office of secretary of state for Ireland, 1580–1608', *IHS*, 35 (2006–7), 137.

53 David Edwards, 'Two fools and a martial law commissioner: cultural conflict and the Limerick assizes of 1606' in idem (ed.), *Regions and rulers in Ireland, 1100–1650: essays for Kenneth Nicholls* (Dublin, 2004), p. 237; idem, 'Ideology and experience: Spencer's *View* and martial law in Ireland' in H. Morgan (ed.), *Political ideology in Ireland, 1541–1641* (Dublin, 1999), p. 127.

54 Patrick Kelly, 'Sir Richard Bolton and the authorship of "A declaration setting forth, and by what means, the laws and statutes of England, from time to time, came to be of force in Ireland", 1644', *IHS*, 35 (2006–7), 1; idem, *'A disquisition touching that great question whether an act of parliament made in England shall bind the kingdom and people of Ireland without their allowance of such act in the kingdom of Ireland', *Anal Hib*, 40 (2007), 17.

the reasons of the Antiquity of those Oppinions; Innovations in the ffundamentals of Government are as Dangerous as in matters of Relligion; the one subverts the Civil the other Ecclesiasticall State, and wee Cannot have a better Plea against Noveltys in both these Prescriptions; *Ab initio non fuit sic*, from the beginning it was not soe.

Rather earlier, in the late 1670s, there had occurred the notorious 'Popish plot'. One Irish angle in the controversies of the period – the role of an Irish informer – has been scrutinized by Gibney.[55]

Moving on a few years, one specific aspect of the victory of William III over James II – the interpretation of the several sets of articles of surrender – has been exposed to fresh analysis from Kinsella.[56] The depth of support for a possible union between Ireland and its larger neighbour as early as 1703 is examined by McGrath,[57] who helpfully reproduces the address to the crown on the question.[58] The same author has also produced a study of the reinterpretation of Poynings' Law in the years between 1692 and 1714.[59]

Two papers touching on aspects of censorship and regulation of the press in the eighteenth century have appeared, Kelly tackling the subject in general terms[60] and Rock focusing on the fears generated in Ireland by the Stamp Act crisis of the mid-1760s.[61]

Turning to the years of the penal laws, it is important to note that the O'Byrne edition of 1981 of the Convert Rolls has recently been reprinted, accompanied by Father Clare's meticulous notes on a proportion of the converts concerned (1,207 in all).[62]

---

55 John Gibney, 'An Irish informer in Restoration England: David Fitzgerald and the "Irish plot" in the Exclusion Crisis, 1679–81', *Éire/Ireland*, 42 (nos. 3 & 4) (2007), 249.
56 Eoin Kinsella, 'In pursuit of a positive construction: Irish Catholics and the Williamite articles of surrender, 1690–1701', *Eighteenth-Century Ireland*, 24 (2009), 11.
57 C.I. McGrath, 'The "Union" representation of 1703 in the Irish House of Commons: a case of mistaken identity', *Eighteenth-Century Ireland*, 23 (2008), 11.
58 Ibid., at 32–5.
59 C.I. McGrath, 'Government, parliament and the constitution: the reinterpretation of Poynings' Law, 1692–1714', *IHS*, 35 (2006–7), 160.
60 James Kelly, 'Regulating print: the State and control of print in eighteenth-century Ireland', *Eighteenth-Century Ireland*, 23 (2008), 142.
61 Suzanne Rock, 'The impact of the Stamp Act crisis, 1765–6 in Ireland', *Irish History*, 1 (2002), 108.
62 *The Convert Rolls: The Calendar of the Convert Rolls, 1703–1838*, ed. Eileen O'Byrne, with Fr. Wallace Clare's annotated list of converts, 1703–78, ed. Anne Chamney (Dublin, IMC, 2005).

The Foxite Whigs at first opposed the Acts of Union of 1800. How and why they finally bowed to the inevitable and accepted that the Acts were a done deal has now been set out at length by Kanter.[63]

At the tail-end of the period of the penal laws there were to be problems regarding religious ceremonies linked to burials in graveyards that were part of the patrimony of the established Church of Ireland. To deal with the problem, the government brought forward its Easement of Burials Bill which became law in 1825 (5 Geo. IV, c. 5). The background to this measure and the story of what happened next have both recently been revisited.[64]

Insight into the First Home Rule crisis of the 1880s is on offer from an edition of a journal kept by an intermediary between Parnell and Dublin Castle.[65]

To move to the twentieth century: political manoeuvrings over the Third Home Rule Bill in the years 1913 and 1914 have been the focus of detailed scrutiny by Smith.[66] The Anglo-Irish Treaty of 1921, predictably enough, continues to attract attention.[67] Post-independence problems arising in the South and which touched on the new constitutional dispensation have included issues as far apart as the Office of the Chief Herald and housing for First World War ex-servicemen. Both have now received attention.[68]

In addition, a series of papers from Mohr has explored a number of more precise constitutional issues linked to the creation of the Irish Free State. His account of the abolition of the appeal to the Judicial Committee of the Privy Council has previously been noted.[69] We now

---

63 Douglas Kanter, 'The Foxite Whigs, Irish legislative independence and the Act of Union, 1785–1806', *IHS*, 36 (2009), 332.
64 J.A. Murphy and Clíona Murphy, 'Burials and bigotry in early nineteenth-century Ireland', *Stud Hib*, 33 (2004–5), 125. See, too, †W.N. Osborough, *Law and the emergence of modern Dublin* (Dublin, 1996), pp 163–8.
65 *Dublin Castle and the First Home Rule crisis: the political journal of Sir George Rottrell, 1884–87*, ed. Stephen Ball (Cambridge, 2008).
66 Jeremy Smith, 'Federalism, devolution and partition: Sir Edward Carson and the search for a compromise on the Third Home Rule Bill, 1913–14', *IHS*, 35 (2007), 496.
67 Claire McGrath, 'The Anglo-Irish treaty, 1921: myths and strategies', *Irish History*, 1 (2002), 5.
68 Noel Cox, 'The Office of the Chief Herald of Ireland and continuity of legal authority', *DULJ*, 29 (2007), 84; Joseph Brady and Patrick Lynch, 'The Irish Sailors' and Soldiers' Trust and its Killester nemesis', *Irish Geography*, 42 (2009), 261; and see below, p. 83.
69 Thomas Mohr, 'The abolition of the Irish appeal to the privy council', *IJ*, 37 (2002), 187. See, too, his broader geographical treatment – 'A British Empire court' – in A. McElligott, L. Chambers, C. Breathnach and C. Lawless (eds), *Power in history* (Historical Studies XXVII) (Dublin and Portland OR, 2011), p. 125.

have this author's views on the foundations for Irish extra-territorial legislation,[70] as well as British involvement in the creation of the Free State Constitution.[71] The challenge posed by the Colonial Laws Validity Act has also been investigated,[72] doubtless a precursor to two further published offerings on British imperial statutes and Irish law.[73] On what is an allied preoccupation – the relationship of the new Free State to the British Empire and Commonwealth – an article by Knirck offers some tentative conclusions.[74]

Moving on to a major event in the history of the Free State in the South, the replacement of the Constitution of 1922 by that of 1937, we have now been furnished with a magisterial volume, amplified by a multitude of original douments, on the background to, and the origins of, the 1937 replacement itself.[75] The miniscule font employed for the footnotes unfortunately detracts from the attractiveness of a volume itself long overdue. A separate essay from the same author considers the Continental inspiration for the document itself.[76]

Censorship in twentieth-century Ireland has continued to attract attention.[77] Martin's foray into the field is a mite unusual, in that he has sought to contrast the different experiences of Northern Ireland and the Irish Free State.[78]

---

70 'The foundations of Irish extra-territorial legislation', *IJ*, 40 (2008), 86.
71 'British involvement in the creation of the Constitution of the Irish Free State', *DULJ*, 30 (2008), 166.
72 'The Colonial Laws Validity Act and the Irish Free State', *IJ*, 43 (2008), 21.
73 'British imperial statutes and Irish law – imperial statutes passed before the creation of the Irish Free State', *Journal of Legal History*, 31 (2010), 299; 'British imperial statutes and Irish sovereignty: statutes passed after the creation of the Irish Free State', *Journal of Legal History*, 32 (2011), 61.
74 Jason Knirck, 'The Dominion of Ireland: the Anglo-Irish Treaty in an Imperial context', *Éire-Ireland*, 42 (nos. 1 & 2) (2007), 229.
75 Gerard Hogan, *The origins of the Irish Constitution, 1928–1941* (Dublin, Royal Irish Academy, 2012). See, too, Micheál Ó Cearúil, *Bunreacht na hEireann: a study of the Irish text* (Dublin, 1999).
76 Gerard Hogan, 'Some thoughts on the origins of the 1937 Constitution' in †Larkin & Dawson (eds), *Lawyers, the law and history*, forthcoming.
77 Kevin Rockett, *Irish film censorship: a cultural journey from silent cinema to internet pornography* (Dublin 2004). On related questions see Mark Finnane, 'The Carrigan Committee of 1930–31 and the "moral condition of the Saorstát"', *IHS*, 32 (2001), 519.
78 Peter Martin, *Censorship in the two Irelands, 1922–1939* (Dublin, 2006). See, too, Caleb Richardson, '"They are not worthy of themselves": *The Tailor and Ansty* debates of 1942', *Éire-Ireland*, 42 (nos. 3 & 4) (2007), 148; Brad Kent, 'The banning of George Bernard Shaw's *The adventures of the black girl in her search for God* and the decline of the Irish Academy of Letters', *Irish University Review*, 38 (2008), 274. Work in this area owes a great deal to Adams' seminal study of 1968 – *Censorship: the Irish experience.*

O'Donoghue has scrutinized an amount of other twentieth-century source material in her attempt to untangle the meaning of so-called 'Irish neutrality'.[79]

A further article from Mohr reconsiders the rights of women under the Free State Constitution.[80] This can be set beside an entire volume devoted to the campaign in Ireland for extending the franchise to women.[81]

We can round off this focus on modern Irish public law by drawing attention to a study of changes implemented in the South in the wake of independence touching the structure of regulation *vis-à-vis* primary and secondary education.[82] Not to be lost sight of either have been Breathnach's fresh study of the Congested Districts Board,[83] and the survey by Cousins of the origins of today's social welfare system in the Republic.[84]

3.5 LEGISLATION

Hansard and its equivalent in assorted parliamentary democracies enables the researcher to find out what legislators said about all manner of things, including legislation scheduled for enactment. Neither in Ireland nor elsewhere was this always the case, full reports of debates, for instance, only becoming *de rigueur* in relatively recent times. So far as the pre-Union Irish parliament is concerned, the *Journals* of the two houses, the Lords and the Commons, which only date from the early seventeenth century, are but of limited value. Much more useful is the *Irish parliamentary register* covering the years from 1781 to 1797 which, as previously noticed, has recently been reprinted.[85] In the last decades of the eighteenth century Irish newspapers began to devote an amount of space to coverage of speeches in parliament, and this source has

79 Aoife O'Donoghue, 'The inimitable form of Irish neutrality: from the birth of the State to World War II', *DULJ*, 30 (2008), 259.
80 Thomas Mohr, 'The rights of women under the Constitution of the Irish Free State', *IJ*, 41 (2006), 20.
81 Louise Ryan and Margaret Ward (eds), *Irish women and the vote: becoming citizens* (Dublin, 2007).
82 John E. Duggan, 'Education and the Catholic Church in the Irish Free State, 1922-32', *Irish History*, 2 (2003), 110.
83 Ciara Breathnach, *The Congested Districts Board of Ireland, 1891–1923: poverty and development in the west of Ireland* (Dublin, 2005).
84 Mel Cousins, *The birth of social welfare in Ireland, 1922–1952* (Dublin, 2003).
85 *The parliamentary register of Ireland, 1781–1797*, 17 vols, with new intro. by W.J. McCormack (Bristol and Tokyo, 1999).

been tapped by Kelly for his extraordinarily useful recapture of debates in the Irish House of Lords.[86]

One legislative battle fought out much earlier in the century – that to secure public backing for the library founded in Dublin by Archbishop Narcissus Marsh – has now been revisited twice, in complementary pieces by Hayton and Osborough.[87] Marsh's tercentenary – it was founded in 1707 – also inspired Hayton to go into a little more detail regarding one element in the membership of the upper chamber – the episcopate.[88]

Kelly, continuing with his programme of casting as much light as it is possible to cast on the workings of the constitution in eighteenth-century Ireland, has produced a study of the role of the Irish privy council in the making of Irish statute-law. A different perspective on eighteenth-century law-making is offered by Osborough with its focus on the legislative lacuna Ireland faced on the coming into force of the Act of Union of 1800 as a result of an inherited 'statute-law deficit'.[89]

One historical conundrum from the sixteenth century – the listing of the prohibited degrees as per the statute book – has been engagingly investigated by Harding.[90]

3.6 THE COURTS

A major publishing event in 2009 was the appearance of volume 125 in the Selden Society's annual series. This volume, a first for Selden, was devoted exclusively to a set of Irish law reports, that put together by

---

86 *Proceedings of the Irish House of Lords, 1771–1800*, ed. James Kelly, 3 vols (IMC, Dublin, 2008).

87 David Hayton, 'Opposition to the statutory establishment of Marsh's Library in 1707: a case-study in Irish ecclesiastical politics in the reign of Queen Anne' in Muriel McCarthy and Ann Simmons (eds), *The making of Marsh's Library: learning, politics and religion in Ireland: 1650–1750* (Dublin, 2004), p. 163; W.N. Osborough, '6 Anne, chapter 19: "setting and preserving a publick library for ever"' in Muriel McCarthy and Ann Simmons (eds), *Marsh's Library: a mirror on the world* (Dublin, 2009), p. 39.

88 D.W. Hayton, 'Bishops as legislators: Marsh and his contemporaries' in McCarthy & Simmons (eds), *Marsh's Library: a mirror on the world*, p. 62.

89 James Kelly, 'The Privy Council of Ireland and the making of Irish law' in Brown & Donlan (eds), *Law and other legalities of Ireland*, p. 47. W.N. Osborough, 'The legislative deficit in eighteenth-century Ireland' in Brown & Donlan (eds), *Law and other legalities of Ireland*, p. 75. One piece of legislation omitted from Osborough's check-list of 'deficits' on the English or British side is now the focus of a full-length study: Susan Mullaney, 'The 1791 Irish Apothecary's Act: the first nationwide regulation of apothecaries in the British Isles', *Eighteenth-Century Ireland*, 25 (2010), 177.

90 Maebh Harding, 'The curious incident of the Marriage Act (no. 2) 1537 and the Irish statute book', *Legal Studies*, 32 (2012), 78.

Henry Singleton (1682–1759), who became the King's prime serjeant in 1726 and chief justice of the Common Pleas in 1740. The collection covers cases argued and determined in the courts of Exchequer and Chancery in Ireland between 1716 and 1734.[91]

As with all Selden Society volumes, the editorial apparatus is of the first importance, and Lyall's exhaustive introduction is no exception. Here we read of the origins of the Irish Exchequer, the development of its different divisions, the changes in substantive law and procedure down the centuries (including development of the *quominus* fiction), and the emergence of the court of Exchequer Chamber. Tackling the cases themselves for the eighteen-year period covered, Lyall deals with the Popery Laws, the Navigation Acts, tithe law, Kerry bonds, and much else besides. That the Irish legal profession during these years in the eighteenth century treated post-1495 English and British legislation as *ipso facto* applicable in Ireland (though never expressly extended to or independently enacted in Ireland) has certainly long been suspected. The first set of Irish law reports to appear in the long interval that separates Sir John Davies' reports of 1615 from the reports of the late eighteenth century now confirms what had thus been suspected. This 640-page volume is likely to provoke a great deal of other questions about the Irish legal system of the period.

Progress in retrieving the history of the court of Chancery in the medieval and early modern periods has been relayed by Crooks.[92] A manuscript in Marsh's Library, MS Z.3.2.17(2), supplies a record of court-martial proceedings held in Dublin for the years 1651–1653 which targeted soldiers of the Dublin garrison as well as ordinary citizens. The manuscript has now been transcribed and is published with a helpful informative introduction from a team of three authors.[93] Interest in the manor courts also continues to be on display. A volume in the Maynooth Studies in Local History series devoted to Dublin's Liberties,[94] though not specifically focused on the courts in the four Dublin liberties – the earl of Meath's (Thomas Court and Donore), the archbishop of Dublin's (St Sepulchre's), the dean and chapter of St Patrick's and the dean and chapter of Christ Church – incorporates an

---

91 *Irish Exchequer Reports, 1716–34*, ed. Andrew Lyall (London, Selden Soc. vol. no. 125, 2009).
92 †Peter Crooks, 'Reconstructing the past: the case of the mediaeval Irish chancery rolls' in Larkin & Dawson (eds), *Lawyers, the law and history* (Dublin, forthcoming).
93 *Heather MacLean, Ian Gentles and Micheál Ó Siochrú, 'Minutes of court martial held in Dublin in the years 1651–3 [with index]', *Anal Hib*, 64 (2011), 56.
94 Kenneth Milne, *The Dublin Liberties, 1600–1850* (Dublin, 2009).

amount of fresh evidence. There is longer, and more detailed concentration on the same courts in an essay from Barnard.[95] The Irish Court of Admiralty is now the focus of a major monograph from Kevin Costello. In addition, two articles dealing with separate aspects of the same court have been produced by him.[96]

One other court has been singled out for attention – the non-jury Special Criminal Court of post-independence southern Ireland.[97] The author furnishes a comprehensive analysis of what has sometimes been viewed as a controversial departure from the common law norm, basing this on the case law, official archives and contemporary criticism.

The experience of non-jury courts in Northern Ireland, introduced in a time of considerable civil unrest, has been the focus of a fresh investigation from Jackson.[98]

3.7 LOCAL GOVERNMENT

Another local authority record book has been published in a modern edition – Byrne's edition of records for Waterford from the mid-fourteenth to the mid-seventeenth century, contained in a volume still extant in the records of the corporation.[99] Of special interest here, perhaps, are the series of records detailing Waterford's trade rivalry with New Ross and the resolutions of 1574 on customary rights enjoyed by the city's then denizens.

All municipal authorities invariably derived a great deal of their revenue both from rents and from miscellaneous tolls and duties. Hill has now described these tolls and duties as collected in Dublin in the eighteenth century and into the early nineteenth.[100]

---

95 T.C. Barnard, 'Local courts in later 17th- and 18th-century Ireland' in Brown & Donlan (eds), *Law and other legalities of Ireland*, p. 33.

96 †Kevin Costello, *The Court of Admiralty of Ireland, 1575–1893* (Dublin, 2011); idem, 'The Court of Admiralty of Ireland, 1745–1756', *AJLH*, l (2008); idem, 'A court "for the determination of causes civil and maritime only": Article 8 of the Act of Union, 1800 and the Court of Admiralty of Ireland' in Brown & Donlan (eds), *Law and other legalities of Ireland*, p. 359.

97 Fergal F. Davis, *The history and development of the Special Criminal Court, 1922–2005* (Dublin, 2007). See, too, M.S. O'Neill, '"In time of "war": Irish domestic security legislation 1939–45', *Irish History*, 2 (2003), 81.

98 John Jackson, 'Many years on in Northern Ireland: the Diplock legacy', *NILQ*, 60 (2009), 213.

99 *The great parchment book of Waterford*, ed. Niall Byrne (Dublin, IMC, 2007).

100 Jacqueline Hill, 'Dublin Corporation and the levying of tolls and customs, *c.*1720–1820' in Brown & Donlan (eds), *Law and other legalities of Ireland*, p. 187.

3.8 LAND USE AND LAND LAW

Whether in Northern Ireland there should be created a national park for the Mournes area is one major political question which has not, as yet, been resolved. The factors that deserve to be taken into account, whatever the eventual decision, have been expertly assembled in a joint study from Bell and Stockdale.[101] As befits the publication in which this study appears, a series of maps conveniently show where there are to be found national parks in Great Britain (fig. 1), such parks in the Irish Republic (fig. 2), and where, back as long ago as 1947, it was suggested such parks might be designated for Northern Ireland (fig. 3). Figure 5 – another map – shows the proposed extent of one model for the Mourne National Park.

In the south of Ireland a programme following independence of rural land redistribution was entrusted to the Irish Land Commission. It was to be pursued with but limited success as Edgeworth has explained in an article with an appropriately evocative title.[102] The Land War of the late nineteenth century has inspired an unusual contribution from Perry Curtis.[103]

J.H. Andrews some twenty-odd years ago drew attention to the dearth of legal commentary on Irish commons and enclosures ('The struggle for Ireland's public commons', in P. O'Flanagan, P. Ferguson and K. Whelan (eds), *Rural Ireland, 1600–1900: modernisation and change* (Cork, 1987)). An attempt to fill the void is now to be found in an article in *Irish Geography*.[104] The author makes use of information secreted in some early Irish nominate law reports, as well as Clare's important short monograph in the Maynooth Studies in Local History series.[105] An appendix purports to list all sixteen parliamentary enclosure Acts for Ireland, only one of which was to be adopted prior to the Act of Union. Crawford has published in the appropriate local history journal an essay on a topic that is not unrelated, and, since it

---

101 Jonathan Bell and Aileen Stockdale, 'Towards a multi-purpose model for the proposed Mourne National Park', *Irish Geography*, 42 (2009), 293.
102 Brendan Edgeworth, 'Rural radicalism restrained: the Irish Land Commission and the courts 1933–39', *IJ*, 42 (2007), 1.
103 L. Perry Curtis, Jr, 'The battering ram and Irish evictions, 1887–90', *Éire-Ireland*, 42 (nos. 3 & 4) (2007), 207.
104 W.N. Osborough, 'Some nineteenth-century Irish litigation over commons and enclosures', *Irish Geography*, 41 (2008), 313.
105 Liam Clare, *Enclosing the commons: Dalkey, the Sugar Loaves and Bray, 1820–1870* (Dublin, 2004).

deals with the Curragh of Kildare, counts as another addition to the growing list of articles on this stretch of land.[106]

The housing of First World War ex-servicemen was provided for by the Irish Sailors' and Soldiers' Land Trust. The fortunes of the trust itself, buffeted by tenants, the courts and the unsympathetic post-independence Free State executive, have now been investigated in an invigorating and original study from Brady and Lynch.[107] The joint authors' conclusion drawn from their investigation merits quotation. The trust, they write,[108]

> made a major contribution to the housing which cannot be gainsaid. It did so via a mechanism which is as fascinating as it is unique, and provides another window on the complex nature of relationships between the British and Irish governments during the period since independence.

The appearance of this timely essay might encourage some researcher to revisit the case law of the 1930s and '40s both in the Free State and in Northern Ireland regarding the position of the Irish Sailors' and Soldiers' Land Trust: *Leggett v. Irish Sailors' and Soldiers' Land Trust* (1932–33), reported at [1945] IR 398, *Casey v. Irish Sailors and Soldiers Land Trust* [1937] IR 208, *Harrington v. Crowley* [1945] IR 393 (all IFS); *Hanna v. Irish Sailors and Soldiers Land Trust* [1936] NI 45. The opportunity, if seized, would enable the researcher also to familiarize himself with the extraordinary opening paragraph of Johnston J.'s judgment in the *Leggett* case in the Irish High Court.

3.9 CIVIL LIABILITY

In the 1920s the writer Brinsley MacNamara published his novel *The valley of the squinting windows*, a none-too-laudatory account of the denizens of the fictional village of Garradrimna. The inhabitants of Delvin, Co. Westmeath, had little difficulty in seeing themselves caricatured in this piece of fiction. The extraordinary outcome was a campaign against the author's father who ran the local school – his

---

106 Hugh Crawford, 'Pasturage on the Curragh', *Journal of the Co. Kildare Archaeological Society*, 20 (2008–9), 92.
107 Joseph Brady and Patrick Lynch, 'The Irish Sailors' and Soldiers' Land Trust and its Killester nemesis', *Irish Geography*, 42 (2009), 261.
108 At 290.

name was Weldon – a campaign led by the local parish priest, a Father Tuite. The upshot was a partially successful boycott, and a reduction in the number of students enrolled, with a resultant loss of income for Weldon. *Weldon v. Tuite* became a remarkable suit in which it was sought to make the defendant answerable for conspiracy. The jury disagreed, and Mr Weldon withdrew from the fray because of the expenditure involved in resuming the legal fight. By 1926 he had retired from his post. The entire saga has now been revisited by Fagan.[109] The essay might not inappropriately be regarded as a companion piece to Osborough's reworking of the events in Callan, Co. Kilkenny in the 1860s and '70s which produced both the defamation case of *O'Keeffe v. Cardinal Cullen* and Thomas Kilroy's novel, *The big chapel* (1971).[110]

3.10 COMMERCIAL LAW

The Ouzel Galley Society came into existence in Dublin early in the eighteenth century, and soon established itself as a vehicle for expeditious, and presumably inexpensive, commercial arbitration. Myths, too, abound concerning the Society: hence Griffith's intriguing essay.[111] Very different in subject matter has been Osborough's examination of the historical origins of the dramatic author's performing right.[112]

3.11 LABOUR LAW

The safety, health and welfare of workers and women teachers and their relations with trade unions have been discussed by Devine and Ó hÓgartaigh respectively.[113]

---

109 Patrick Fagan, '*The Valley of the squinting windows*: background to a novel', *Ríocht na Midhe*, 18 (2007), 220.
110 W.N. Osborough, 'Another country, other days: revisiting Thomas Kilroy's *The big chapel*', *Irish University Review*, 32 (2002), 39. See, too, Colin Barr, *The European culture wars in Ireland: the Callan Schools Affair, 1868–81* (Dublin, 2010).
111 Lisa Marie Griffith, 'The Ouzel Galley Society in the 18th century: arbitration body or drinking club' in Brown & Donlan (eds), *Law and other legalities of Ireland*, p. 165.
112 W.N. Osborough, 'Chapters from the history of the dramatic author's performing right', *DULJ*, 33 (2011), 10.
113 Francis Devine, 'Safety, health and welfare at work in the Irish Free State and the Republic of Ireland, 1922–90: measuring the problem', *Saothar*, 31 (2006), 65; Margaret Ó hÓgartaigh, 'Female teachers and professional trade unions in early twentieth-century Ireland', *Saothar*, 29 (2004), 33.

3.12 CHARITIES LAW

Church briefs, an inheritance from the pre-Reformation church, furnished a makeshift system of charitable relief, via authorized house-to-house collections, until they were abolished in the 1820s. Their employment as a means of compensation for victims of major fires in two Ulster towns – Enniskillen and Lisburn – in the early 1700s is now examined by Osborough.[114]

The relationship between medical provision and charity in the eighteenth century and part of the nineteenth is the focus of a study from Geary[115] that constitutes an overdue contribution to the social history of medicine in the country.

3.13 CRIME AND CRIMINAL JUSTICE

Fresh insight into the administration of criminal justice in nineteenth- and early twentieth-century Ireland is on display in a magisterial volume in the Irish Legal History Society series.[116] Focusing on murder trials, Vaughan, the author, takes us through the entire process from arrest and committal to trial and sentence. Final chapters tackle applications for the exercise of the prerogative of mercy and execution of the sentence ('death by hanging'). Throughout, care has been taken to avail of all the key sources of information – including what is to be found in the law reports as well as in the parliamentary papers and in the Convict Reference Files in the Irish National Archives. Vaughan's extensive bibliography features six pages of 'Contemporary Works' and five of 'Modern Works'; it is strongly recommended to researchers anxious to deepen their knowledge of the entire subject. McMahon has been ploughing a somewhat similar furrow. Besides editing a volume concentrating on comparative aspects of crime and criminal justice in a pan-European context,[117] in which he has a paper on the prosecution of Irish homicide,[118] McMahon elsewhere has addressed himself to

---

114 W.N. Osborough, 'Early eighteenth-century charitable relief for two fire-damaged Ulster towns' (forthcoming).
115 Laurence M. Geary, *Medicine and charity in Ireland, 1718–1851* (Dublin, 2004).
116 †W.E. Vaughan, *Murder trials in Ireland, 1836–1914* (Dublin, 2009). See, too, *Infanticide in the Irish Crown files at assizes, 1883–1900*, ed. Elaine Farrell (Dublin, IMC, 2012).
117 Richard McMahon (ed.), *Crime, law and popular culture in Europe, 1500–1900* (Cullompton, Devon and Portland, OR, 2008).
118 '"The fear of the vengeance": the prosecution of homicide in pre-Famine and Famine Ireland' in McMahon (ed.), *Crime, law and popular culture*, p. 138.

homicide statistics[119] and the operation of the prerogative of mercy[120] for the first half of the nineteenth century. Garnham, for his part, has asked important questions of the pattern of Irish criminal justice in the eighteenth century.[121] The repudiation by the Irish Exchequer Division in the late 1880s of English precedent reducing, via the writ of certiorari, judicial superintendence of magistrates' court decisions, wrote an important chapter in late nineteenth-century Irish criminal justice administration. This variation between Irish and English doctrine was brought to an end in the key adjudication of *R. (Martin) v. Mahony* [1910] 2 IR 695. The episode has now been engagingly rescrutinized by Kevin Costello.[122]

Studies of individual criminal trials remain a popular focus of research effort. Invariably, such studies shed light on both substantive law and criminal procedure. Turvey has revisited the trial and condemnation, in the reign of Elizabeth I, of Sir John Perrot[123] (a precedent revisited in 1916 in the case of Sir Roger Casement),[124] and Edwards, that of the martial law commissioner, John Downing, in 1606 (previously signalled).[125] In addition, among the papers delivered at a bicentenary symposium on the life and legacy of Robert Emmet was one from Mr Justice Hardiman of today's Irish Supreme Court on Emmet's celebrated trial before Lord Norbury in 1803.[126] It was, Hardiman contended, a show trial with an outcome predetermined to serve the political needs of the government and erstwhile anti-unionist lawyers. After 1798, and in the wake of Viscount Kilwarden's murder, the result, naturally enough, was predictable. Daniel O'Connell's involvement in the Magee trials of 1813 has also been scrutinized by

---

119 '"A violent society"? Homicide rates in Ireland, 1831–1850', *IESH*, 31 (2009), 1.
120 '"Let the law take its course": punishment and the exercise of the prerogative of mercy in pre-Famine and Famine Ireland' in Brown & Donlan (eds), *Law and other legalities of Ireland*, p. 133.
121 Neal Garnham, 'The limits of English influence on the Irish criminal law, and the boundaries of discretion in the 18th-century Irish criminal justice system' in Brown & Donlan (eds), *Law and other legalities of Ireland*, p. 97.
122 '*R. (Martin) v. Mahony*: the history of a classical certiorari authority', *Journal of Legal History*, 27 (2006), 267.
123 Roger Turvey, *The treason and trial of Sir John Perrot* (Cardiff, 2005).
124 See *Rex v. Casement* [1917] 1 KB 98 at 118 (argument of the Crown).
125 David Edwards, 'Two fools and a martial law commissioner: cultural conflict at the Limerick assize of 1606' in idem (ed.), *Regions and rulers in Ireland, 1100–1650: essays for Kenneth Nicholls* (Dublin, 2004), p. 237; above, p. 71.
126 In Anne Dolan, P.M. Geoghegan and Darryl Jones (eds), *Reinterpreting Emmet: essays on the life and legacy of Robert Emmet* (Dublin, 2007), at p. 227.

Geoghegan.[127] The same Magee had been a protagonist in an earlier quarrel dealt with by Greene and signalled above.[128]

The Maynooth Studies in Local History series had previously included titles focusing on notorious individual homicide cases from the nineteenth century.[129] The editorial practice has been continued, fresh titles in recent times concentrating on murders in Co. Cork in 1823,[130] in Co. Roscommon in 1847,[131] and in Co. Monaghan in 1851.[132] The burnings at Wildgoose Lodge in Co. Louth in 1816, the focus of considerable early attention, are now revisited by Dooley in a monograph entirely devoted to them.[133] More general surveys of aspects of agrarian unrest for both the eighteenth and nineteenth centuries have emanated from the pens of Patterson, Kelly and Donnelly, Jr.[134] The victim of one of the most notorious of the late nineteenth-century murders – in Co. Donegal in 1878 – that of the 3rd earl of Leitrim is now the subject of a typically masterly biography from Malcomson.[135] Forms of urban protest, we need reminding, have not been entirely ignored.[136]

Interest in the history of local gaols continues to be expressed.[137] One penal institution, no longer with us, has been the focus of fresh analysis – the Irish borstal, located until 1956 in cramped quarters in

127 Patrick Geoghegan, 'Daniel O'Connell and the Magee trials, 1813' in Brown & Donlan (eds), *Law and other legalities of Ireland*, p. 283.
128 See above, p. 72.
129 E.g., Frank Sweeney, *The murder of Conell Boyle, County Donegal, 1898* (Dublin, 2002).
130 D.A. Cronin, *Who killed the Franks family? Agrarian violence in pre-Famine Cork* (Dublin, 2009).
131 Padraig Vesey, *The murder of Major Mahon, Strokestown, Co. Roscommon, 1847* (Dublin, 2008).
132 Michael McMahon, *The murder of Thomas Douglas Bateson, Monaghan, 1851* (Dublin, 2006).
133 Terence Dooley, *The murders at Wildgoose Lodge: agrarian crime and punishment in pre-Famine Ireland* (Dublin, 2007).
134 James G. Patterson, 'Republicanism, agrarianism and banditry in the west of Ireland, 1798–1803', *IHS*, 35 (2006), 17; Jennifer Kelly, 'A study of Ribbonism in Co. Leitrim in 1841', *Irish History*, 2 (2003), 32; James S. Donnelly, Jr, 'Captain Rock: ideology and organization in the Irish agrarian rebellion, 1821–24', *Éire-Ireland*, 42 (nos. 3 & 4) (2007), 60.
135 A.P.W. Malcomson, *Virtues of a wicked earl: the life and legend of William Sydney Clements, 3rd earl of Leitrim, 1806–78* (Dublin, 2008).
136 See Martyn Powell, 'Ireland's urban houghers; moral economy and popular protest in the late eighteenth century' in Brown & Donlan (eds), *Law and other legalities of Ireland*, p. 231.
137 Stan J. O'Reilly, 'Tales from Wicklow Gaol: murder, confinement and escape', *Wicklow Historical Society*, 3 (no. 6) (2007), 32; 3 (no. 7) (2008), 8.

the former local prison in Clonmel.[138] The building itself no longer survives, though it served as an all-Ireland institution from its opening in 1906 down to Partition. As regards prisons themselves, Rogan has furnished a ground-breaking study on the introduction in the South of new Prison Rules in 1947.[139] For the nineteenth century McCarthy has essayed to present a general perspective.[140] And another prison diary – from Belfast and for a relatively recent period – has been edited.[141] A memoir of years spent in an industrial school in the west of Ireland has also seen the light of day.[142]

A recent volume has seen its authors cast their eyes over the entire range of institutions in which over the first fifty years of Irish independence what can be termed 'coercive confinement' was in vogue – psychiatric hospitals, mother and baby homes, Magdalen laundries, reformatory and industrial schools, prisons and borstal.[143]

Assorted offerings from McCracken, Campbell, McKenna and Regan have helped to tease out aspects of the story of the Royal Irish Constabulary in its final decades.[144] The role of the Irish policeman in the policing of the British Empire and Commonwealth has not been ignored either.[145] How women police came to be introduced in the Republic in 1957 has now also been told by Shepard.[146] The challenge faced by the police in dealing with different forms of threat to society has also been exposed to special scrutiny.[147]

138 Conor Reidy, *Ireland's 'moral hospital': the Irish borstal system, 1906–1956* (Dublin, 2009).
139 Mary Rogan, 'The Prison Rules, 1947: political imprisonment, politics and legislative change in Ireland', *IJ*, 43 (2008), 89.
140 John-Paul McCarthy, '"In hope and fear": the Victorian prison in perspective', *Irish History*, 1 (2002), 119.
141 *The insider: the Belfast prison diaries of Eamonn Boyce, 1956–1962*, ed. Anne Bryson (Dublin, 2007).
142 Peter Tyrrell, *Founded on fear: Letterfrack Industrial School, war and exile*, ed. Diarmuid Whelan (Dublin, 2006).
143 Eoin O'Sullivan and Ian O'Donnell, *Coercive confinement in Ireland: patients, prisoners and penitents* (Manchester, 2012).
144 D.P. McCracken, *Inspector Mallon: buying Irish patriotism for a five-pound note* (Dublin, 2009); Fergus Campbell, 'The social composition of the senior officers of the Royal Irish Constabulary', *IHS*, 36 (2009), 522; *A beleagured station: the memoir of Head Constable John McKenna, 1891–1921*, ed. John McKenna (Belfast, 2009); *The memoirs of John M. Regan: a Catholic officer in the RIC and RUC, 1909–1948*, ed. Joost Augusteijn (Dublin, 2007).
145 Georgina Sinclair, 'The "Irish" policeman and the Empire: influencing the policing of the British Empire/Commonwealth', *IHS*, 36 (2008), 173.
146 Christopher Shepard, 'A liberalisation of Irish social policy? Women's organisations and the campaign for women police in Ireland, 1915–57', *IHS*, 36 (2009), 564.
147 Aoife Bhreatnach, 'Policing the community: homicide and violence in Traveller and settled society', *IESH*, 34 (2007), 47. See, too, Maria Luddy, *Prostitution and Irish society* (Cambridge, 2007).

3.14 THE JUDICIARY

In his Selden Society volume, *Irish Exchequer Reports, 1716–34*, Dr Lyall furnishes biographical notes on the judges and lawyers who figure in them – individuals such as Henry Singleton himself, Viscount Midleton LC, Lord Wyndham LC, Chief Baron Marlay, and Barons St Leger and Wainwright. Room too is also found for Gorges Edmond Howard, Eaton Stannard, Cornelius Callaghan and Jonathan Swift's *bête noire*, Serjeant Bettesworth.

In addition, those seeking detailed information on the sundry Irish legal luminaries of the past are now in the fortunate position of being able to consult the sixty volumes of the *Oxford dictionary of national biography* (previously signalled), but also, as a result of publication in 2009, the 9 volumes of the *Dictionary of Irish biography*. The future Mr Justice Wylie has been the focus of separate treatment from Marshall.[148]

Bardic eulogies in Irish paying tribute to judges of the common law dispensation are rare but not unknown. One such was composed by Dáibhí Ó Bruadair in honour of Chief Justice John Keating over the acquittal of Catholics at the Limerick spring assizes in 1682 – 'Searc na suadh an chrobhaing chumhra' ('Love of sages in the fragrant cluster').[149] In 1597, nearly a century before, Nicholas Walsh became chief justice of the Common Pleas, and he, too, was the recipient of a bardic encomium. The poem itself, the background, and the quite extraordinary factual problem presented that required a juridical solution, have all now been discussed by McManus.[150] Two of the quatrains in which Walsh's talents are eulogized may appropriately be set down here:

> Breath chlaon ar chumha ná ar chrodh an Giuisdís Bhails ní bhéarudh acht firbhreath niamhghlan nach náir do mhínleach chiallmhur chomhráidh.
>
> (Justice Walsh would not give a corrupt judgment for any consideration of wealth; his, rather, is a true pure blameless judgment from the best of intellectual discourses.)
>
> (quatrain 14)

148 †R.D. Marshall, 'Lieutenant W.E. Wylie KC: the soldiering lawyer of 1916' in Larkin & Dawson (eds), *Lawyers, the law and history*, forthcoming.
149 *Duanaire Dháibhidh Uí Bhruadair* (Irish Texts Society xiii) (London, 1913).
150 Damian McManus, 'Niall Frosach's "Act of truth": a bardic apologue in a poem for Sir Nicholas Walsh, Chief Justice of the Common Pleas (†1615)', *Ériu*, 58 (2008), 133.

> Meanma ar mhnáibh biatach do-bheir Giuisdís Bhails, bláth an dligheidh; do-bheir mná meirleach ag gul, i lá a dheighbhreath do dhearbhudh.

> (When his excellent judgments are pronounced Justice Walsh, flower of the law, brings hope to the wives of farmers; to the wives of thieves, however, he brings despair.)

(quatrain 18)

Coming much closer to the present times, a new generation of scholarship has started to tackle themes linked to the history of the judicial branch in the early decades of the independent Irish state. Aside from the work of Mohr to which reference is made above,[151] particular interest attaches to such surveys as that penned by Coffey on the early Free State judiciary,[152] and that penned by Hogan on the plan hatched in the 1930s for a Constitutional Court.[153] Other research for the same period has been in progress for some time; the results are likely to be published over the next few years.

Very different in nature has been the topic of judicial dress down the centuries. Martin has now broached the subject in modern times so far as the middle-ranking courts are concerned.[154] A text of 1879 on petty sessions courts and the duties of their clerks has been examined by Osborough.[155]

3.15 LEGAL PROFESSION

Interest in the legal profession in the early modern period and indeed later, an interest inspired by the late Donal Cregan, has continued to attract a number of researchers. Ohlmeyer's focus has rested on recusant lawyers in the reign of Charles I.[156] McGrath, on the other

---

151 Above, pp 76–7.
152 D.K. Coffey, 'The judiciary of the Irish Free State', *DULJ*, 33 (2011), 61.
153 Gerard Hogan, 'John Hearne and the plan for a Constitutional Court', *DULJ*, 33 (2011), 75.
154 † John A.H. Martin, 'Reflections on judicial dress with particular reference to the county and circuit courts' in Larkin & Dawson (eds), *Lawyers, the law and history*, forthcoming.
155 W.N. Osborough, 'The Dublin Castle career (1866–78) of Bram Stoker', *Gothic Studies*, 1:2 (1999), 222.
156 Jane Ohlmeyer, 'Irish recusant lawyers in the reign of Charles I' in M. Ó Siochrú (ed.), *Kingdom in crisis: Ireland in the 1640s* (Dublin, 2001), p. 63.

hand, has sought to cover a longer period and has been religion-neutral.[157]

Returning to the position exclusively of Catholics, the period between the Restoration of Charles II in 1660 and the flight of James II from London in 1688 witnessed a marked upsurge in the admission of Catholics – an interval now covered in depth by Maynard.[158] With the accession of William and Mary a perceptible hardening occurred – Catholics in Ireland being excluded from the bar by an English Act of 1692 (3 Will. & Mary II, c. 2) and in England by another English Act, one of 1696 (7 & 8 Will. III, c. 24). These legislative provisions had the effect of inducing a number of Catholics to conform to the Church of Ireland, but others were to remain Catholic, becoming 'chamber counsel', lawyers who did not plead at the bar but specialized in conveyancing. This group is the subject of detailed consideration by Bergin.[159] One of the Catholics in question, Dennis Molony (1650–1726), had a substantial library, and this also has been described by Bergin, in conjunction with Chambers.[160]

Lawyers' libraries back in Ireland, as it chanced, had also been the subject of brief attention. Boran discusses the library of the judge Jerome Alexander bequeathed to Trinity College Dublin in 1670 – see TCD MS MUN/LIB/10/28, ff. 1r–9r – as well as that of Christopher Sexton, an early seventeenth-century lawyer from Limerick (not, alas, listed in *King's Inns admission papers, 1607–1867*) – see BL Add. MS 19865, ff. 74–8;[161] and Barnard has taken note of some lawyers' libraries of later years, in the eighteenth century.[162] Kenny has written about his discovery of a rare edition of Cicero's orations in the King's Inns library.[163]

157 Brid McGrath, 'Ireland and the third university: attendance at the Inns of Court, 1603–1649' in Edwards (ed.), *Regions and rulers in Ireland*, p. 217.
158 Hazel Maynard, 'The Irish legal profession and the Catholic revival, 1660–89' in C.I. McGrath et al. (eds), *People, politics and power: essays on Irish history 1660–1850 in honour of James I. McGuire* (Dublin, 2009), p. 28.
159 John Bergin, 'The Irish Catholic interest at the London inns of court, 1674–1800', *Eighteenth-Century Ireland*, 24 (2009), 36.
160 †John Bergin and Liam Chambers, 'The library of Dennis Molony (1660–1726), an Irish Catholic lawyer in London', *Anal Hib*, 41 (2009), 83.
161 Elizabethanne Boran, 'Libraries and collectors, 1550–1700' in *The Irish book in English (The Oxford history of the Irish book – iii)*, ed. Raymond Gillespie and Andrew Hadfield (Oxford, 2006), p. 91 at pp 98–9.
162 Toby Barnard, 'Libraries and collectors, 1700–1800' in *The Irish book in English*, ed. Gillespie & Hadfield, p. 111 at pp 128–30.
163 †Colum Kenny, 'On lawyers, their obligations and the Cicero collection at King's Inns Library' in Larkin & Dawson (eds), *Lawyers, the law and history*, forthcoming.

Some useful information on early women barristers and solicitors on both sides of the Irish border has been brought together by Ó hÓgartaigh.[164]

Two prominent Irish barristers and cases with which they were associated have been brought into focus by Geoghegan[165] and Lord Hutton.[166]

The story of the move of the King's Inns from their ruined and abandoned base on the Liffey to their new home, still extant, at the top of Dublin's Henrietta Street on Constitution Hill, has been revisited in welcome detail by Kenny.[167] The breach with King's Inns and the establishment of the Inn of Court of Northern Ireland have been revisited by Hart.[168]

A handsome new volume from Hewitt deals in depth with the history of the solicitors' profession in Northern Ireland.[169] Careers of John Rea and Blair Mayne will be found here, interspersed with accounts of the old Northern Law Club, an excellent collection of photographs and even details of questions asked of candidates at the preliminary examination in 1928. Papers set then, Hewitt sagely observes, could well have stretched some of today's lawyers (p. 27): e.g., 'Quote some typical lines from either Herrick or Cowper and mention what you consider is most distinctive of each author'.

Two academic lawyers of distinction to have recently died – Robert Heuston and John Kelly – have received entries in the *Dictionary of Irish biography*. Paul O'Higgins, who died in 2008, has been recalled in the pages of the *Northern Ireland Legal Quarterly*.[170]

The Law School of Trinity College aside, the history of the other university law schools has hitherto been unresearched, and thus unsung. Amends are now being made, with essays from O'Malley and

164 'Antonia MacDonnell, Meath's first female barrister and the legal profession in the early twentieth century', *Ríocht na Midhe*, 20 (2009), 273.
165 †Patrick Geoghegan, 'Daniel O'Connell and the law' in Larkin & Dawson (eds), *Lawyers, the law and history*, forthcoming.
166 †Lord Hutton, 'Sir Edward Carson K.C. and the Archer-Shee case' in Larkin & Dawson (eds), *Lawyers, the law and history*, forthcoming.
167 Colum Kenny, '"By no means relished by the gentlemen of the bar": the King's Inns moves to Constitution Hill' in Gillian O'Brien and Finola O'Kane (eds), *Georgian Dublin* (Dublin 2008), p. 78.
168 †A.R. Hart, 'Kings Inns and the foundation of the Inn of Court of Northern Ireland – the northern perspective' in Larkin & Dawson (eds), *Lawyers, the law and history*, forthcoming.
169 Alan Hewitt, *The Law Society of Northern Ireland: a history* (Belfast, 2010).
170 J.F. McEldowney, 'Paul O'Higgins (1927–2008)', *NILQ*, 59 (2008), 245.

Osborough, dealing, respectively, with NUI Galway (University College, Galway) and University College, Dublin.[171]

3.16 COURTHOUSES

The history of Irish courthouses continues to attract a modest degree of attention, less perhaps than one might expect given the abundance of source-material, however scattered that turns out to be. In a study devoted to buildings in a single county – Armagh – Brett deals with the courthouse in Armagh city itself, as well as smaller edifices in Loughgall and in Lurgan, where the courthouse was to be converted into a public house.[172] Duffy, in a biography of James Gandon,[173] deals at some length with the construction of Dublin's Four Courts and the controversies surrounding it: in the main, the trouble Gandon faced at the hands of the likes of James Malton, Col. William Burton Conyngham, and, later, Lord Redesdale. The work on preparing the site finally got under way early in 1786, at which point we are privileged, thanks to Duffy, to have preserved for us this evocative description of the workmen at what was then taking place:[174]

> Half-starved and clad in ragged clothes, many in bare feet, they laboured to feed their families at all costs. During the first week in March, the streets were deep in slush and half-frozen snow, and in this bitter weather the foundation stone for the Four Courts was laid.

3.17 LAW REPORTING

Elsewhere in this additional bibliographical essay, mention is made of the major event of 2009 – the publication in the Selden Society series of *Irish Exchequer Cases, 1716–34*, in essence a transcription of MS 71 of the Singleton Collection at Columbia University in New York. This

---

171 L. O'Malley, 'Law' in Tadhg Foley (ed.), *From Queen's College to National University: essays towards an academic history of QCG, UCG, NUI Galway* (Dublin, 1999), p. 16; W.N. Osborough, 'The [U.C.D.] law school's early professoriate', *IJ*, 46 (2011), 1. O'Malley's lengthy (108pp) essay constitutes a veritable *tour de force*.
172 C.E.B. Brett, *Buildings of Co. Armagh* (Belfast, 1999).
173 Hugo Duffy, *James Gandon and his times* (Kinsale, Co. Cork, 1999).
174 Ibid., at p. 187.

collection of reports on miscellaneous topics helps to fill the gap that separates Sir John Davies' Irish reports of 1615 from the late eighteenth century when Irish law reporting was finally established on a permanent footing. This key development in publishing came too late, alas, to be taken note of in Hall's magisterial survey of Irish law reporting which had previously been noted.[175] On Davies, on the other hand, there has come a fresh assessment of his career and the place of his law reports both in terms of law reporting generally and of Irish legal history.[176]

3.18 AN EPILOGUE

An essay in the public press to mark the ninetieth anniversary of what occurred in Dublin on 30 June 1922 serves to remind us, finally, of the difficulties posed for a truly comprehensive and convincing portrait of the legal history of this island by the destruction of so many of the country's legal records by the explosion and fire at the Dublin Record Office in the Four Courts complex.[177] Herbert Wood (later to be Deputy Keeper), as previously signalled, published three years before this destruction the records then known to be in the State's guardianship.[178] This invaluable *Guide* today naturally requires to be compared with contemporaneous and subsequent accounts of actual records which for one reason or another were to survive the conflagration.[179] It is well to be reminded at the same time that there are serial collections of some material originating in initiatives taken mainly in the nineteenth century (both in England and here) that assist in plugging many of the gaps in our understanding that remain.[180]

An essay I published in 1990 reflects generally on the state of the surviving records – why so much has been lost though some records remain – and it, too, I venture to suggest, might be consulted for

---

175 E.G. Hall, *The superior courts of law: 'official' law reporting in Ireland, 1866–2006* (Dublin, 2007).
176 Paul Brand, 'Sir John Davies: law reporter or self-publicist', *IJ*, 43 (2008), 1.
177 Catriona Crowe, 'Ruin of Public Record Office marked loss of great archive', *Irish Times*, 30 June 2012.
178 H. Wood, *A guide to the records deposited in the Public Record Office of Ireland* (Dublin, HMSO, 1919).
179 H. Wood, 'The destruction of the Public Records', *Studies*, 11 (1922), 363; M. Griffith, 'A short guide to the Public Record Office of Ireland', *IHS*, 8 (1952–53), 45.
180 W.N. Osborough, 'Legal history: confronting the challenge' in T. Mohr and J. Schweppe (eds), *Thirty years of legal scholarship* (Dublin, 2011), p. 142 at pp 142–3.

guidance and, conceivably – though this is something immodest to claim – for inspiration as well. The piece was entitled 'In search of Irish legal history: a gap for explorers'.[181] I repeat here the final paragraph,[182] which ends on an uplifting note:

> In *Pilgrim's Progress* the progress of Christian and his wife Christiana is interrupted by a succession of traveller's nightmares. There is the Slough of Despond to cross and the Valley of Humiliation to pass through. Earlier there had been the encounter with Doubting Castle and its inhabitants, Giant Despair and his wife Diffidence. The journey of the Irish legal history explorer is punctuated likewise by the appearance on the horizon of landmarks equally calculated to cause dismay, disillusionment and – certainly where the deliberate destruction of source-material can be vouched for – even dread. But those obstacles, I would contend, though formidable, can be surmounted, for, if the analogy with John Bunyan's masterpiece is permissible – and plainly it should not be stretched too far – there is a Promised Land and it beckons all the time: 'After this, I beheld until they were come unto the Land of Beulah, where the sun shineth night and day'.

---

181 *Long Room: Bulletin of the Friends of the Library, Trinity College Dublin*, 35 (1990), 28.
182 Ibid., at 36.

The inauguration of the Irish Legal History Society

The text of the inaugural lecture of the Irish Legal History Society, by W.N. Osborough, delivered in the Provost's House, Grafton Street, Dublin, on 12 February 1988, in the presence of the Chief Justice of Ireland, the Hon. T.A. Finlay, and the Lord Chief Justice of Northern Ireland, the Rt. Hon. Lord Lowry.

Alexander Knox, in his history of County Down, published in 1875, describes an excursion he had recently made to a deserted graveyard in the parish of Slanes in Upper Ards:

> At the time of my visit, a workman was engaged in deepening the fading letters on an old tombstone, to preserve a little longer, from total oblivion, the memory of some obscure name...[1]

The image is an arresting one, and possibly conveys something of the character of the enterprise upon which the new Irish Legal History Society that is being formally inaugurated today is about to embark. Our aim can indeed be expressed in such modest terms – to seek to preserve a little longer from total oblivion the memory of the legal past of this island. Over time and with the benefit of experience it is to be hoped nevertheless that the Society may become a good deal more ambitious.

Comparisons should act as the spur. England has boasted a legal history society since 1887 – the Selden, named after John Selden, the prominent legal antiquarian of seventeenth-century England. And Scotland has possessed a legal history society, named after Viscount Stair, the celebrated Scots institutional writer of the later seventeenth century, since 1934.

It is appropriate to point out on an occasion such as this that the two societies – the Selden and the Stair – have down the years served as a

---

[1] Alexander Knox, *A history of the county of Down* (Dublin, 1875), p. 472.

meeting-ground for the practising and academic branches of the legal profession in both England and Scotland. Both societies, it hardly needs to be added, have an outstanding record in extending the knowledge and appreciation of legal history in their respective jurisdictions. The new Irish Legal History Society might profitably seek merely to emulate the achievements of these two legal history societies on the neighbouring, larger island. The mood in which it should set out to do so has been expressed in apt language, albeit applied to a different context, by the director of the archaeological excavations at Sutton Hoo in East Anglia. Placed on the defensive by critics of the cost of the present programme of excavation, Professor Martin Carver was recently quoted as having issued the following retort:

> Every generation needs a prestige project, performed in deliberation rather than haste, to improve our ability to make sense of the past.[2]

In something of the self-same spirit, may I commend to you this afternoon the objectives of the Irish Legal History Society?

There are many uses to which the study of legal history may be applied, a study to which the new Society can be counted upon to lend its support. There is no need to rehearse all of them here. The legal records of the past constitute an immense reservoir of information on how people in bygone times have 'lived and moved and had their being'. There is a vividness of detail which on occasion proves wholly engrossing. From the reservoir of information as to daily life in medieval Ireland that is to be found in the *Calendars of Justiciary Rolls* and in the Armagh archiepiscopal registers, let me allude to just one case that is dealt with in the former. In 1307 an adulterer in Youghal, with the name of Stephen Oregan, fell into a trap set for him by the woman's husband, John Dun, and his relations. When caught, Stephen was to be castrated – hence the proceedings before the Justiciar, John Wogan, in Cork that are reported in the *Justiciary Rolls*.[3] The accompanying detail, the methods adopted by Stephen and Basilia (vainly as it turns out) to avoid detection – their bribery of servants, their moving around in bare feet and in the dark – and how finally the trap was sprung, marks a considerable advance on the hackneyed plots served up by today's writers of television soap operas, non obstante the continuing saga in the BBC's *Eastenders* of Lofty and Michelle.

2   *Irish Times*, 30 December 1985.
3   *Calendar of Justiciary Rolls Ireland, 1305–7*, pp 376–7.

But the study of legal history has rewards that go very much further. 'A lawyer without history or literature', Sir Walter Scott observes through the lips of Counsellor Pleydell in his novel *Guy Mannering*,

> is a mechanic, a mere working mason; if he possesses some knowledge of these, he may venture to call himself an architect.[4]

Despite the touch of hyperbole, clearly there is more than a grain of truth in Pleydell's philosophy. The historical dimension to legal study undoubtedly contributes to a depth and to a breadth of understanding. Sometimes indeed it may fairly be said that the historical dimension is essential to any understanding at all. And no one in the profession, be he judge, practitioner or academic, naturally is in the position to predict what will be the next legal conundrum to cross his path where a familiarity with certain matters historical might not prove a positive boon. The adage that knowledge is power applies with peculiar force in the case of apt historical knowledge in the possession of the lawyer.

Recourse to nineteenth-century learning may turn out to be all that is required. Where an increasing number of young barristers and solicitors may not be able to identify the functions of the old grand juries or answer correctly when the latter came to an end, this is plainly challenge enough. How much greater the challenge where the subject-matter is treasure trove or the wardship in lunacy jurisdiction or the title to Lough Neagh,[5] and the voyage of discovery that becomes mandatory to enable the particular modern problem to be solved in a convincing and not merely a perfunctory fashion obliges us to navigate in some very strange waters indeed where charts are in short supply or non-existent.

Like the hydrographic survey, the Irish Legal History Society will be in the business of supplying charts – and, let me add, by way of parenthesis, at what we think is the bargain annual rate of £30, or £28 sterling. This will be realized by means of the publishing programme that is now projected. One very general observation is in order: the time-span will be deliberately wide. We would hope eventually to cover the ground from the days of the early Irish law tracts, down through 'the first adventure of the common law' to the legal and constitutional

---

4 Ch. 37.
5 *Webb v. Ireland* [1988] ILRM 565; *In re Midland Health Board* [1988] ILRM 251; *Toome Eel Co. (N. Ireland) Lcd v. Cardwell* [1963] N.I. 92, [1966] N.I. 1.

developments of the early twentieth century. Turning to the particular, we would hope to be able to reprint the small number of classic works of Irish legal history. More important, in a sense, however, we would encourage the transcribing and editing of surviving manuscript Irish court records and reports and aim to print previously unpublished collections of Irish legislation – the seventeenth-century Irish government proclamations, the Acts of James II's Patriot Parliament of 1689, the Decrees of Dáil Éireann 1919–22. In 1989 we anticipate that we will be in a position to commence our series of volumes with a collection of essays on various aspects of the history of the Irish legal profession. I am happy to say that for this initial volume a team of a dozen or so authors has already been assembled.

The backing of historians and archivists and of the Irish legal community for what is afoot is clearly of the first importance. And here I should like to express the Society's thanks for the financial help that has been received to date. But the guarantee of success must be the calibre of the work that is put into the Society's early volumes. As to that I personally have no reservations. I consider the intellectual manpower is there; the enthusiasm and, I venture to believe, the interest too are there. Accordingly, it must be regarded as an opportune moment to initiate this new Society.

In the nineteenth century, a succession of stalwart individuals made it their business to care for Ireland's legal and other public records, and to publicize their existence – people such as William Lynch, William Betham, Bartholomew Duhigg, James Hardiman and John Gilbert. A personal favourite is James Ferguson whose remarkable career is told in Prendergast's introduction to Haliday's *The Scandinavian kingdom of Dublin*. What John O'Donovan and Eugene O'Curry represented so far as the early Irish law tracts were concerned, this too, to a degree, was what Ferguson represented so far as the records of the courts of common law, and especially Exchequer, were concerned – he was a 'gallant pioneer' in their transcription and study. The new Legal History Society will face many difficulties in the years ahead. One episode from Ferguson's career can usefully be recalled – to give us the courage we will need. Aware that some medieval Irish plea rolls were being advertised for sale by a dealer in antiquarian manuscripts in Germany, Ferguson applied to a succession of members of the Irish government and Irish judiciary of the day for a grant in aid of purchase. His endeavours met with no success, whereupon Ferguson himself set forth for the Continent and acquired the items in question out of his own pocket.[6] They were later added to the collection removed to the Public Record Office and there they remained until the conflagration of 1922 destroyed both them and so much else besides.

Among those solicited unavailingly by Ferguson was Thomas Langlois Lefroy. The latter had been an early beau of Jane Austen's, but sagacious relatives had managed to separate them. Lefroy returned to Ireland where a notable career in politics and law awaited him – as did the implacable hostility of O'Connell. It was as Chief Justice of the Queen's Bench that Lefroy, who was to hold this office into his ninetieth year, turned Ferguson down flat.[7] For that sin of omission, that instant of thoughtlessness, that peccadillo, I am certain by now that the chief judicial dignitaries of Ireland in the intervening years – whatever their titles and their constitutional and political loyalties – have done ample penance. If only to let the *lares* and *penates* rest content, it is time, I sense, on this most suitable of occasions, to wipe the slate clean and, formally and unconditionally, welcome them in from the cold. In the light of the endorsements that the Chief Justice of Ireland and the Lord Chief Justice of Northern Ireland have been generous enough to extend to the aims of the Irish Legal History Society, but more especially in view of their joint presence here this afternoon actually to inaugurate the Society, it gives me very great pleasure indeed to be able to do so.

---

6 Charles Haliday, *The Scandinavian kingdom of Dublin*, ed. with some notice of the author's life by J.P. Prendergast (2nd ed., Dublin, 1884; repr. Shannon, 1969), preface, pp xxviii–xxix.
7 Ibid.

A tribute to Nial

A speech given by Professor Norma Dawson, president of the Irish Legal History Society, at a dinner held in Dublin on 27 May 2011 in honour of Professor W.N. Osborough, founder of the Society, to mark the occasion of his retirement from the Council of the Society

We are here to honour our very good friend, Nial, the founder of the Irish Legal History Society, and to express our thanks for his exceptional – *unique* – service as a member of Council. When he intimated his decision to retire from Council, I think it is fair to say that we all felt completely bereft.

The record does not show when Nial first conceived the idea of establishing a legal history society for Ireland, but it does show that he took the first step towards its creation about 25 years ago this autumn, when he sent out copies of a memorandum entitled '*A proposal to found a society to advance the study of Irish legal history*'. One of those who received the memorandum was Professor Desmond Greer, then in his second term of office as Dean of Faculty in Queen's. Rather fortuitously, Des recently gave me some of his Irish Legal History Society papers, including a file of correspondence from those early days.

By letter dated 16 February 1987, Nial reported to Des that he had completed a round of correspondence and in some cases visits with a number of people in eight categories – judges, barristers, solicitors, university lawyers, university historians, public records staff, archivists, and librarians. He had also had some fruitful exchanges with the Selden and Stair Societies. The overwhelming response to his proposal, he said, was enthusiastic, but – Nial notes in his letter to Des:

> A few of those to whom I wrote were frankly dubious. The line they took was roughly as follows: I am not a philistine. Most of my contemporaries are, however. And there may not be a snowball's chance in hell that the initiative would ever get off the ground.

(Little did he know when he penned that letter of 16 February 1987 that he was simultaneously providing the material for an after-dinner speech to be given in his honour on 27 May 2011: such is the power of legal history.)

Undeterred by a small number of doubters, Nial proceeded to Step 2 in the foundation of the Society – the establishment of a steering group to draft a constitution, address the financing and administration of the society, arrange publicity, and plan a publishing programme which was to be the Society's principal *raison d'être*. Daire Hogan, Colum Kenny and John Larkin were early and enthusiastic adherents to the cause, as was Mr Justice Costello who took the chair at the first meeting of the steering group in April 1987. By the end of 1987, a constitution had been prepared, a publicity leaflet printed, many practical matters addressed, and an executive committee formed – the first Council.

Everything was now in place for Step 3 – the formal inauguration of the Society on 12 February 1988 at a ceremony held in the Provost's House, Trinity College Dublin, with Mr Justice Costello as the first president, Daire Hogan as honorary treasurer and Nial as honorary secretary, a position that he was to hold until his election as president in 2000. 1988 also saw the appointment of two vice-presidents; one of whom was Tony Hart.

All of this was promoted and superintended in every particular by Nial. The Society up and running, he turned his attention to the publication programme, having already identified possible contributors for the Society's impressive first volume, *Brehons and attorneys: studies in the history of the Irish legal profession*. Co-edited by Nial and Daire Hogan, this was published in 1990 by Irish Academic Press, the Society's then publisher of choice – the first of a list of now 20 books published under the imprimatur of the Society, now in association with Four Courts Press. At the recent launch of Kevin Costello's *The Court of Admiralty of Ireland, 1575–1893*, it occurred to me how fitting it was that volume no. 20 in the ILHS series – which somehow seems like a milestone in our publication history – should be published by one of Nial's protégés, one of a group of outstanding young legal historians to emerge from UCD, each with their own story to tell of Nial's influence as a teacher and colleague.

The reputation that attends our publishing programme has until only very recently rested almost entirely on Nial's unstinting contribution as literary editor of the Society for almost two decades.

No succeeding literary editor has been or ever will be able to match his contribution in terms of time, energy and expertise. But he set such high standards that the possibility of having a book published under our aegis continues to attract authors worth publishing.

It is impossible in the course of a few minutes to do justice to Nial's contribution as founder, secretary, president and council member. Particular highlights were the tenth anniversary conference held at Queen's, and the joint British/Irish legal history conference held in University College Dublin in July 2003, the culmination of Nial's presidency. Put briefly, Nial's contribution has been immense, visionary, inspiring and enduring.

And as fellow council members, have we not each individually benefited from his unique brand of witty warmth and friendship, and the extraordinary generosity with which he has dealt with our own requests – pleas! – for information or advice on some point of legal history. How often chatting to him over a cup of tea at a book launch or a meeting, have I longed to ditch the tea and take out my notebook and pen and write down everything that he says. And I have, more than once, spent half an hour on the Enterprise bound for Belfast doing just that.

A particular delight is his trade mark style of providing just so much specific information to satisfy the enquirer before ending with some cryptic, even oracular remark, the purpose of which seems to be to make the enquirer go and do some work of her own. His letter of 16 February 1987 to Des Greer is a case in point. It concludes with the following:

> Incidentally, whilst on these matters, in the collection of Maitland's letters edited by Fifoot ...[1] you will be able to read the extraordinary and tragic tale of what befell Selden's first honorary secretary and treasurer, P.E. Dove. I certainly did not know it all before.

I do not know if Des ever took the bait, but I found myself in Queen's library earlier this week reading the volume in question. The story told there, somewhat obliquely, of Mr Dove is one of lust, greed, corruption and self-destruction, which left Frederic Maitland lamenting the threatened demise of his 'beloved Selden'. Happily, the

---

1 F.W. Maitland, *Letters*, ed. C.H.S. Fifoot (Cambridge, MA, 1965).

Irish Legal History Society's choice of first honorary secretary has brought us nothing but prosperity, success and distinction.

Nial – for imagining that there might be a legal history society for Ireland; for overcoming all obstacles to found and establish the Irish Legal History Society, for leading and guiding the Society since its inception, for everything that you have done for us collectively and individually, thank you. Might you do one more thing for us? We ask you please to accept our nomination as honorary life member, with our heartfelt thanks and every good wish for the future. Ladies and gentlemen, the toast is – Nial.

Norma Dawson

Index of authors

A barrister (H.H. Joy?)
    Letter to the rt hon Lord Lyndhurst, on the appointment of sheriffs in Ireland, under the earl of Mulgrave, 17n

Adams, Michael
    Censorship, the Irish Experience, 78n

Andrews, J.H.
    'The struggle for Ireland's public commons', 82

Appleby, J.
    Calendar of material relating to Ireland from the High Court of Admiralty examinations, 43n
    'Merchants and mariners, pirates and privateers: an introductory survey of the records of the High Court of Admiralty as a source for regional maritime history', 43n

Appleby, J., and O'Dowd, M.
    'Cahir O'Doherty and the *Dove* of Cartemyne 1603–4: a sidelight on Gaelic admiralty jurisdiction', 43n
    'The Irish Admiralty: its organisation and development, *c*.1570–1640', 26, 30, 43

Augusteijn, Joost (ed.)
    The memoirs of John M. Regan: a catholic officer in the RIC and RUC, 1909–1948, 88

Austin, V.A.
    'The ceili and the Public Dance Halls Act 1935', 41

Bade, E.S.
    'A princely judgment (the earl of Ormond's case)', 26n

Baker, J.H.
    'United and knit to the imperial crown: an English view of the Anglo-Hibernian constitution in 1670', 41

Ball, F.E.
    The judges of Ireland, 1221–1921, 14

Ball, J.
    A policeman's Ireland: recollections of Samuel Waters, RIC, 54

Ball, Stephen (ed.)
    Dublin Castle and the First Home Rule crisis: the political journal of Sir George Rottrell, 1884–87, 76n

Barnard, Toby C.
    Cromwellian Ireland: English government and reform in Ireland, 1649–1660, 18, 24, 25, 30, 37
    'Lawyers and the law in late seventeenth-century Ireland', 57

'Libraries and collectors, 1700–1800', 91
'Local courts in later 17th- and 18th-century Ireland', 80–1
Barnes, J.
Irish industrial schools, 1868–1908: origins and development, 55n
Barry, Judith
'Sir Geoffrey Fenton and the office of secretary of state for Ireland, 1580–1608', 74
Bartlett, T.
The fall and rise of the Irish nation: the Catholic question, 1690–1830, 39n
Bartlett, T., and Hayton, D.W. (eds)
Penal era and golden age: essays in Irish history, 1690–1800, 20
Barton, B.
From behind a closed door: secret court-martial records of the 1916 Easter Rising, 41
Beames, M.R.
'Rural conflict in pre-Famine Ireland: peasant assassination in Tipperary, 1837–47', 52
Beckett, J.C.
'Anglo-Irish constitutional relations in the later eighteenth centry', 21
Bell, Jonathan, and Stockdale, Aileen
'Towards a multi-purpose model for the proposed Mourne National Park', 82
Bergin, John
'Poynings' Law in the eighteenth century', 39n
'The Irish Catholic interest at the London inns of court, 1674–1800', 91
Bergin, John, and Chambers, Liam
'The library of Dennis Molony (1660–1726), an Irish Catholic lawyer in London', 91
Bhreatnach, Aoife
'Policing the community: homicide and violence in Traveller and settled society', 88
Binchy, D.A.
Corpus Iuris Hibernici, 66
Bolton, G.C.
The passing of the Irish act of union, 20, 39–40
Bonsall, P.
The Irish RMs: the resident magistrates in the British administration of Ireland, 44, 61
Boran, Elizabethanne
'Libraries and collectors, 1550–1700', 91
Bourke, A.
The burning of Bridget Cleary: a true story, 51
Boyce, D.G.
'British conservative opinion, the Ulster question and the partition of Ireland, 1919–21', 21
Boyce, D.G., Eccleshall, R., Geoghegan, V. (eds)
Political thought in Ireland since the seventeenth century, 38n
Boylan, H.
Dictionary of Irish biography, 31
Boyle, C.K., 32

Boyle, K.
  'Police in Ireland before the union', 29–30
  'The Tallents report on the Craig-Collins pact of 30 March 1922', 22
Bradshaw, B.
  The dissolution of the religious orders in Ireland, 31
  The Irish constitutional revolution of the sixteenth century, 20
Brady, J.C.
  'Legal developments, 1801–79', 19, 27, 37, 46n
  Religion and the law of charities in Ireland, 27–8
Brady, Joseph, and Lynch, Patrick
  'The Irish Sailors' and Soldiers' Land Trust and its Killester nemesis', 76n, 83
Brand, P.
  'Ireland and the literature of the early common law', 32n
  'Irish law students and lawyers in late medieval Ireland', 55n
  'Sir John Davies: law reporter or self-publicist', 94
Bray, Gerald (ed.)
  Records of Convocation: xvi Ireland, 1101–1690; xvii Ireland 1690–1869 (Part 1): xviii Ireland 1690–1869 (Part 2), 70
Breathnach, Ciara
  The Congested Districts Board of Ireland, 1891–1923: poverty and development in the west of Ireland, 78
Breatnach, Liam
  A companion to the Corpus Iuris Hibernici, 66
  'Law', 68n
  'Lawyers in early Ireland', 68
  'On the original extent of the Senchas Már', 68n
  'The first third of Bretha Nemed Toísech', 67n
  Uraicecht na Ríar: the poetic grades in early Irish law, 67
Bretherton, George
  'Irish inebriate reformatories, 1899–1920: an experiment in coercion', 54
Brett, C.E.B.
  Buildings of Co. Armagh, 93
  Courthouses and market-houses of the province of Ulster, 62
  'Two eighteenth-century provincial attorneys: Matthew Brett and Jack Brett', 56n–57n
Bric, M.J.
  'The tithe system in eighteenth century Ireland', 25, 45
Bridgeman, Ian
  'The constabulary and the criminal justice system in nineteenth-century Ireland', 53
Broeker, G.
  Rural disorder and police reform in Ireland, 1812–36, 29
Brown, M., Geoghegan, P.M., and Kelly, J. (eds)
  The Irish Act of Union: bicentennial essays, 40n
Brown, Michael, and Donlan, S.P. (eds)
  The Law and other legalities of Ireland, 1689–1850, 72n, 73n, 79n, 81n, 84n, 86, 86n, 87n

Brupbacher, O., et al. (eds)
  Remembering and forgetting: yearbook of legal history, 67n
Bryson, Anne (ed.)
  The insider: the Belfast prison diaries of Eamonn Boyce, 1956–1962, 88n
Buckley, J.F.
  'Legal publishing', 63
Bull, P.
  'The significance of the nationalist response to the Irish land act of 1903', 47
Burke, H.
  The people and the poor law in nineteenth-century Ireland, 42
Byrne, Margaret
  'The Law Society library', 57
Byrne, Niall (ed.)
  The great parchment book of Waterford, 81

Caldicott, C.E.J. (ed.)
  'Patrick Darcy, an Argument', 38, 64
Calendar of Justiciary Rolls Ireland, 1305–7, 97
Calendar of State Papers, Ireland, 25n, 70
Callanan, F.
  T.M. Healy, 58n
  'T.M. Healy: the politics of advocacy', 58n
Campbell, C.
  Emergency law in Ireland, 1918–1925, 38
Campbell, Fergus
  'The social composition of the senior officers of the Royal Irish Constabulary', 88
Campbell, J.
  As I was among the captives: prison diary, 1922–1923, 55n
  Prisoners: the Civil War letters of Ernie O'Malley, 55n
Carey, John
  'An edition of the pseudo-historical prologue to the Senchas Már', 67
  'The testimony of the dead', 68n
  'The two laws in Dubthach's judgment', 68
Carey, T., 54
  Mountjoy: the story of a prison, 54
Carroll-Burke, P.
  Colonial discipline: the making of the Irish convict prison, 54, 54n
Casey, D.J.
  'Wildgoose Lodge: the evidence and the lore', 52n
Casey, J.P.
  'The genesis of the Dáil courts', 19, 44n
  The Irish law officers, 58
  The office of the attorney general in Ireland, 22
  'Republican courts in Ireland, 1919–1922', 19, 44n
Charles-Edwards, T.M.
  'A contract between king and people in early medieval Ireland? Crith Gablach on kingship', 68n

Early Irish and Welsh kinship, 68n
'Early Irish law', 66
'The construction of the Hibernensis', 68n
'The pastoral role of the church in the early Irish laws', 68n
Charles-Edwards, T.M., Owen, Morfydd E., and Walters, D.B. (eds)
  Lawyers and lawmen: studies in the history of law presented to Professor Dafydd Jenkins on his 75th birthday, 69n
Chart, D.A. (ed.)
  The register of John Swayne, archbishop of Armagh, 1418–1439, 70
Clancy, F.G.
  'The Irish penitentials', 68
Clare, Liam
  Enclosing the commons: Dalkey, the Sugar Loaves and Bray, 1820–1870, 82n
Clark, S., and Donnelly Jr, J.S. (eds)
  Irish peasants: violence and political unrest, 1780–1914, 52
Clarke, A.
  'The history of Poynings' Law, 1615–1641', 20
  'The policies of the "Old English" in parliament, 1640–41', 21
Clayton, M.C. (ed.)
  The Council Book for the province of Munster, c.1599–1649, 72
Cochrane, Nigel
  'The policeman's lot is not a happy one: duty, discipline, pay and conditions in the Dublin Metropolitan Police, c.1838–45', 53
Coffey, D.K.
  'The judiciary of the Irish Free State', 90
Cohen, M.L.
  'Irish influences on early American law books: authors, printers and subjects', 63
Collette, C.
  'So utterly forgotten: Irish prisoners and the 1924 Labour Government', 55n
Comerton, E.A.
  A handbook of the Magistrates' Courts Act (N.I.) 1964, 27
Conley, C.A.
  'Irish criminal records, 1865–1892', 55
Connolly, P. (ed.)
  Irish Exchequer payments, 1270–1446, 69
  Statute rolls of the Irish parliament, Richard III–Henry VIII, 64n
Connolly, S.J.
  'Albion's fatal twigs: justice and law in the eighteenth century', 50n
  'Jacobites, Whiteboys and Republicans: varieties of disaffection in eighteenth-century Ireland', 52n–53n
  'Law, order and popular protest in early eighteenth-century Ireland: the case of the Houghers', 50n
  Religion, law and power: the making of Protestant Ireland, 1660–1760, 50n
  'The Houghers', 50n
  'Violence and order in the eighteenth century', 50n
Connolly, S.J. (ed.)
  Political ideas in eighteenth-century Ireland, 38n

Corish, P.J.
'Catholic marriage under the penal code', 28
Cosgrove, A.
Marriage in Ireland, 28
'Marriage in medieval Ireland', 28
Cosgrove, A., and McGuire, J.I. (eds)
Parliament and community: historical studies XIV, 20
Costello, C. (ed.)
The Four Courts: 200 years – essays to commemorate the bicentenary of the Four Courts, 62
Costello, F.
'The Republican courts and the decline of British rule in Ireland, 1919–21', 44n
Costello, K.
'A court "for the determination of causes civil and maritime only": Article 8 of the Act of Union, 1800 and the Court of Admiralty of Ireland', 81
The Court of Admiralty of Ireland, 1575–1893, 81, 102
'The Court of Admiralty of Ireland, 1745–1756', 81
The law of habeas corpus in Ireland, 41
'*R. (Martin) v. Mahony*: the history of a classical certiorari authority', 86
'Sir William Petty and the court of Admiralty in Restoration Ireland', 43, 60
Cousins, Mel
The birth of social welfare in Ireland, 1922–1952, 78
Cowman, Des
'Combination, conflict and control: colliers and quarrymen in Tipperary, 1825–45', 48
Cox, Noel
'The Office of the Chief Herald of Ireland and continuity of legal authority', 76
Crawford, Hugh
'Pasturage on the Curragh', 82–3
Crawford, J.G.
Anglicizing the government of Ireland: the Irish privy council and the expansion of Tudor rule, 1556–1578, 38
'The origins of the court of castle chamber: a star chamber jurisdiction in Ireland', 24–5, 42
A star chamber court in Ireland – the court of Castle Chamber, 1571–1641, 37n, 42–3
Cregan, D.F.
'Irish Catholic admissions to the English inns of court, 1558–1625', 31, 57n
'Irish recusant lawyers in politics in the reign of James I', 31, 57
Cronin, D.A.
Who killed the Franks family? Agrarian violence in pre-Famine Cork, 87
Crooks, Peter
'Reconstructing the past: the case of the mediaeval Irish chancery rolls', 80
Crossman, V.
'Emergency legislation and agrarian disorder in Ireland, 1821–41', 52n
Local government in nineteenth-century Ireland, 42

Index of authors

Crowe, Catriona
   'Ruin of Public Record Office marked loss of great archive', 94
Cullen, L.
   'Catholics under the penal law', 40
Cunningham, Bernadette (ed.)
   Calendar of State Papers Ireland, Tudor period 1566–1567, revised edition, 70
Curran, C.P.
   'Figures in the Hall', 62
Curtis, E.
   'The courtbook of Esker and Crumlin, 1592–1600', 26n
Curtis, E., and McDowell, R.B. (eds)
   Irish historical documents, 1172–1922, 13n
Curtis, L.P., Jr
   'The battering ram and Irish evictions, 1887–90', 82
   Coercion and conciliation, 30
   'Landlord responses to the Irish land war 1877–1887', 47

Daly, M.
   'Irish nationality and citizenship since 1922', 41
D'Arcy, D.
   'The Dublin police strike of 1882', 54
D'Arcy, F.A.
   'The decline and fall of Donnybrook Fair: moral reform and social control in nineteenth-century Ireland', 53
D'Arcy, F.A., and Hannigan, K. (eds)
   Workers in union, documents and commentaries on the history of Irish labour, 48n
Darcy, P.
   An argument ..., edited by C.E.J. Caldicott, 38, 64
   An argument delivered ... by the express order of the House of Commons, 17, 38
Davies, W., and Fouracre, P. (eds)
   The settlement of disputes in early medieval Europe, 67
Davis, Fergal F.
   The history and development of the Special Criminal Court, 1922–2005, 81n
Davitt, C.
   'Civil jurisdiction of the courts of the Irish republic, 1920–1922', 19
Dawson, N., 47
   'Illicit distillation and the revenue police in Ireland in the eighteenth and nineteenth centuries', 30
Dawson, N., Greer, D., and Ingram, P. (eds)
   One hundred and fifty years of Irish law, 47n
Day, E.B.
   Mr Justice Day of Kerry: a discursive memoir, 60n
Delany, V.T.H.
   Christopher Palles (1831–1920), 30
   'The history of legal education in Ireland', 32
   'Legal studies in Trinity College, Dublin since the foundation', 32
   'Lord Justice Christian and law reporting: a sidelight on Irish legal history', 32
   'The palatinate court of the liberty of Tipperary', 26

Delany, V.T.H., and Delaney, D.R.
  The canals of the south of Ireland, 29
Devine, Francis
  'Safety, health and welfare at work in the Irish Free State and the Republic of Ireland, 1922–90: measuring the problem', 84
Devlin, J., and Clarke, H.B. (eds)
  European encounters: essays in memory of Albert Lovett, 57n
Dickson, D., Keogh, D., and Whelan, K. (eds)
  The United Irishmen, 39n
Dictionary of Irish biography, 31, 59, 89, 92
Dictionary of national biography, 31, 59
Dolan, Anne, Geoghegan, P.M., and Jones, Darryl (eds)
  Reinterpreting Emmet: essays on the life and legacy of Robert Emmet, 86
Donaldson, A.G.
  Some comparative aspects of Irish law, 14
Donlan, S.P. (ed.)
  Sullivan, F.S., *Lectures on the constitution and laws of England with a commentary on Magna Carta, etc.*, 64
Donnelly, James S., Jr
  'Captain Rock: ideology and organization in the Irish agrarian rebellion, 1821–24', 87
Dooley, Terence, 54
  The murders at Wildgoose Lodge: agrarian crime and punishment in pre-Famine Ireland, 87
Dowling, J.A., 47
  'The genesis of Deasy's Act', 47
  'Of ships and sealing wax; the introduction of land registration in Ireland', 47n
  'Under which King, Bezonian? Succession to the Hertford Irish estates in 1870', 47
  'The Irish Court of Appeal in Chancery 1857–77', 44n, 47n
  'The Landed Estates Court, Ireland', 44n, 47
Dudley, R.
  'Fire insurance in Dublin, 1700–1860', 49
  'The rise of the annuity company in Dublin 1700–1800', 49
Duffy, Hugo
  James Gandon and his times, 93
Duggan, John E.
  'Education and the Catholic Church in the Irish Free State, 1922–32', 78
Dunne, M., and Philips, B.
  The courthouses of Ireland: a gazetteer of Irish courthouses, 62

Edgeworth, Brendan
  'Rural radicalism restrained: the Irish Land Commission and the courts 1933–39', 82
Edwards, David
  'Ideology and experience: Spencer's *View* and martial law in Ireland', 74n
  'Two fools and a martial law commissioner: cultural conflict at the Limerick assizes of 1606', 71, 74, 86

Edwards, David, and Empey, Adrian
   'Tipperary liberty ordinances of the "black" earl of Ormond', 70–1
Edwards, R.D., and Moody, T.W.
   'The history of Poynings' Law: part I', 20n
Edwards, R.D. and O'Dowd, M.
   Sources for early modern Irish history, 1534–1641, 14n
Ellis, E., and Eustace, P. Beryl
   Registry of Deeds (Dublin), Abstracts of wills, vol. 3: 1785–1832, 45
Ellis, S.G.
   Reform and Revival: English government in Ireland, 1470–1534, 15, 24, 35–6
   Tudor Ireland: crown, community and the conflict of cultures 1470–1603, 15, 24
Empey, C.A.
   'Medieval Knocktopher, a study in manorial settlement – II', 26–7

Fagan, P.
   Divided loyalties: the question of the oath for Irish Catholics in the eighteenth century, 40
   '*The Valley of the squinting windows:* background to a novel', 84
Falkiner, C.L.
   'The parliament of Ireland under the Tudor sovereigns', 20n
Farrell, B.
   'The drafting of the Irish Free State constitution', 22
Farrell, B. (ed.)
   The Irish parliamentary tradition, 20
Farrell, Elaine (ed.)
   Infanticide in the Irish Crown files at assizes, 1883–1900, 85n
Farrell, S.
   'Recapturing the flag: the campaign to repeal the Party Processions Act, 1860–72', 41n
Faughnan, S.
   'The Jesuits and the drafting of the Irish constitution of 1937', 42n
Federowicz, K.
   'The problems of disbandment: the RIC and imperial migration, 1919–29', 54
Ferguson, K.
   'A portrait of the Irish bar, 1868–1968', 58
Ferguson, K. (ed.)
   King's Inns barristers, 1868–2004, 58
Fifoot, C.H.S. (ed.)
   F.W. Maitland, *Letters*, 103
Finnane, M.
   'The Carrigan Committee of 1930–31 and the "moral condition of the Saorstát"', 77n
   Insanity and the insane in post-famine Ireland, 29
   'Irish crime without the outrage: the statistics of criminal justice in the later nineteenth century', 55
Fleming, D.A. and Malcomson, A.P.W. (eds)
   A volley of execrations: the letters and papers of John Fitzgibbon, earl of Clare, 1772–1802, 59

Foxton, David
   Revolutionary lawyers: Sinn Féin and Crown Courts in Ireland and Britain, 1916–1923, 73
Frame, R.
   'The medieval Irish keepers of the peace', 27

Gallagher, M.
   'The presidency of the republic of Ireland: implications of the "Donegan" affair', 22
Garnham, N.
   The courts, crime and the criminal law in Ireland, 1692–1760, 50
   'Criminal legislation in the Irish parliament, 1692–1760', 50n
   'How violent was eighteenth-century Ireland?', 50, 53
   'The limits of English influence on the Irish criminal law, and the boundaries of discretion in the 18th-century Irish criminal justice system', 86
   'The short career of Paul Farrell: a brief consideration of law enforcement in eighteenth-century Dublin', 50n
   'The trials of James Cotter and Henry, Baron of Santry: two case studies in the administration of criminal justice in early eighteenth-century Ireland', 50n
Geary, L.M.
   Medicine and charity in Ireland, 1718–1851, 85
   The plan of campaign, 1886–91, 46n
Genet, J., and Hellegouarc'h, E. (trans.)
   Discours sur la sujétion de l'irlande, 64n
Geoghegan, Patrick M.
   'Daniel O'Connell and the law', 92
   'Daniel O'Connell and the Magee trials, 1813', 86–7
   1798 and the Irish Bar, 57
   The Irish act of Union: a study in high politics, 1798–1801, 40n
Gerriets, Marilyn
   'Theft, penitentials and the compilation of the early Irish laws', 68
Gibbons, S.R.
   Captain Rock, night errant: the threatening letters of pre-Famine Ireland, 1801–45, 51
Gibney, John
   'An Irish informer in Restoration England: David Fitzgerald and the "Irish plot" in the Exclusion Crisis, 1679–81', 75
Gillespie, R.
   'A manor court in seventeenth-century Ireland', 43–4
   'Women and crime in seventeenth-century Ireland', 50n
Gillespie, R., and Moran, G. (eds)
   Longford: essays in county history, 44n
Golding, G.M.
   George Gavan Duffy, 1882–1951, 30
Graham, B.J., and Hood, S.
   'Town tenant protest in late nineteenth and early twentieth century Ireland', 47
Graham, E.
   'Religion and education: the constitutional problem', 22

Grattan, Sheena
   'Of pin-money and paraphernalia, the widow's shilling and a free ride to Mass: one hundred and fifty years of property for the Irish wife', 47
Greene, J.C.
   'The trials of Richard Daly and John Magee, involving the Sham Squire, the Lottery Swindle of 1788, the Billiard Marker's Ghost, and the Grand Olympic pig hunt', 72, 87
Greer, D.S.
   'Crime, justice and legal literature in nineteenth-century Ireland', 63–4
   'The development of civil bill procedure in Ireland', 49n
   'A false mawkish and mongrel humanity? The early history of employers' liability in Ireland', 48n
   'Lawyers or politicians? The Irish judges and the right to vote, 1832–1850', 41
   'Middling hard on coin: truck in Donegal in the 1890s', 48
   'A security against illegality? The reservation of crown cases in nineteenth-century Ireland', 44
Greer, D.S., and Mitchell, V.A.
   Compensation for criminal damage to property, 28
Greer, D.S., and Nicolson, J.W.
   The Factory Acts in Ireland, 1802–1914, 48
Griffin, B.
   The Bulkies: police and crime in Belfast, 1800–1865, 53
   'Prevention and detection of crime in nineteenth-century Ireland', 53
   Sources for the study of crime in Ireland, 1801–1921, 55n
Griffith, Lisa Marie
   'The Ouzel Gallery Society in the 18th century: arbitration body or drinking club', 84
Griffith, M.
   'A short guide to the Public Record Office of Ireland', 94n

Haliday, Charles (ed.)
   The Scandinavian kingdom of Dublin, 99, 100n
Hall, E.G.
   The Superior Courts of law: official law reporting in Ireland, 1866–2006, 65, 94
Hall, E.G., and Hogan, D. (eds)
   The Law Society of Ireland, 1852–2002: portrait of a profession, 56–7, 63
Hamilton, A.
   'A treatise on impressing', 237
Hamilton, J.B. (ed.)
   Records of the court leet, manor of Dunluce, Co. Antrim, held in Ballymoney, 26
Hand, G.J.
   'The common law in Ireland in the 13th and 14th centuries: two cases involving Christ Church, Dublin', 69n
   'The Irish military establishment from the restoration to the union', 21
   'A reconsideration of a German study of the Irish constitution of 1922', 31
   'Rules and orders to be observed in the proceedings of causes in the high court of chancery in Ireland, 1659', 24
Hand, G.J. (ed.)
   The report of the Irish boundary commission 1925, 21

Hand, G.J., and Treadwell, V.W.
    'His majesty's directions for ordering and settling the courts within the kingdom of Ireland, 1622', 17, 37
Hardiman, Adrian
    'Law, crime and punishment in Bloomsday Dublin', 73
    'The trial of Robert Emmet', 86
Hardiman, James, 99
    History of Galway, 13
    A Statute of the Fortieth year of King Edward III enacted in a parliament held in Kilkenny, A.D. 1367, 13
    Tracts Relating to Ireland, II, 13, 31–2
Harkness, D.
    'The difficulties of devolution: the post-war debate at Stormont', 22
Harris, F.W.
    'The commission of 1609: legal aspects', 17
    'Matters relating to the indictments of "the fugitive earls and their principal adherents"', 17
    'The rebellion of Sir Cahir O'Doherty and its legal aftermath', 17
Harrison, R.S.
    Irish insurance: historical perspectives, 1650–1939, 49n
Hart, A.R.
    'Audley Mervyn: lawyer or politician?', 57n
    'Fighting Fitzgerald – mad, bad and dangerous to know: an eighteenth-century murder trial', 51
    A history of the king's serjeants at law in Ireland: honour rather than advantage?, 57
    'Kings Inns and the foundation of the Inn of Court of Northern Ireland – the northern perspective', 92
Hawkins, R.
    'Dublin castle and the Royal Irish Constabulary (1916–22)', 30
    'Government *versus* secret societies: the Parnell era', 30
Hay, D., Linebaugh, P., Rule, J.G., Thompson, E.P., and Winslow, C. (eds)
    Albion's fatal tree: crime and society in eighteenth-century England, 50
Hayton, David
    'Bishops as legislators: Marsh and his contemporaries', 79
    'Opposition to the statutory establishment of Marsh's Library in 1707: a case-study in Irish ecclesiastical politics in the reign of Queen Anne', 79
Hayton, David (ed.)
    Letters of Marmaduke Coghill, 1722–1738, 59
Heaney, H.
    'Ireland's penitentiary, 1820–1831; an experiment that failed', 29, 54
Hempton, D., and Hill, M.
    'Godliness and good citizenship: evangelical Protestantism and social control in Ulster, 1790–1850', 53
Henry, B.
    'Industrial violence, combinations and the law in late eighteenth-century Dublin', 48
Henry, B. (ed.)
    'Animadversions on the street robberies in Dublin, 1765', 51

Henry, P.L.
   'A note on the Brehon law tracts of procedure and status, Cóic Conara Fugill and Uraicecht Becc', 68
Herlihy, J.
   The Dublin Metropolitan Police: a short history and genealogical guide, 54
   The Dublin Metropolitan Police: alphabetical list of officers and men, 54
   The Royal Irish Constabulary: a short history and genealogical guide, 54
   The Royal Irish Constabulary: alphabetical list of officers and men, 54
   Royal Irish Constabulary officers: a biographical dictionary and genealogical guide, 1816–1922, 54
Heuston, R.F.V.
   Essays in constitutional law, 23
   'Hugh McCalmont Cairns (1819–82), judge', 31
   'James Shaw Willes (1814–72), judge', 30
Hewitt, Alan
   The Law Society of Northern Ireland: a history, 92
Hickey, E.
   Irish law and lawyers in modern folk tradition, 65
Hill, Jacqueline
   'Dublin Corporation and the levying of tolls and customs, c.1720–1820', 81
   'The intelligentsia and Irish nationalism: the 1840s', 31, 32
Hinde, R.S.E.
   'Sir Walter Crofton and the reform of the Irish convict system', 29
Hirst, C.
   Religion, politics and violence in nineteenth-century Belfast: the Pound and Sandy Row, 53
Hogan, D.
   'Arrows too sharply pointed: the relations of Lord Justice Christian and Lord O'Hagan', 60n
   The legal profession in Ireland, 1789–1922, 32, 56
   'R.R. Cherry, lord chief justice of Ireland 1914–1916', 60n
   'Vacancies for their friends: judicial appointments in 1866–1867', 60
Hogan, D., and Osborough, W.N. (eds)
   Brehons, serjeants and attorneys: studies in the history of the Irish legal profession, 56n, 102
Hogan, Gerard, 62
   'Chief Justice Kennedy and Sir James O'Connor's application', 61
   'John Hearne and the plan for a Constitutional Court', 90
   The origins of the Irish Constitution, 1928–1941, 77
   'Some thoughts on the origins of the 1937 Constitution', 77
Holland, A.C.
   'The papers of Hugh Kennedy: a research legacy for the foundation of the State', 61
Holloway, I.
   '*O'Connell v. The Queen:* a sesquicentennial remembrance', 51n
Holmes, C.
   'The British government and Brendan Behan, 1941–1952: the persistence of the Prevention of Violence Act', 42n

Howlin, Niamh
  'Controlling jury composition in nineteenth-century Ireland', 73
  'English and Irish jury laws: the growing divergence, 1825–1833', 73
  'Merchants and esquires: special juries in Dublin, 1725–1833', 73
Hughes, J.L.J.
  'The Dublin court of conscience', 27
Hutton, Lord
  'Sir Edward Carson KC and the Archer-Shee case', 58, 92

Inglis, B.
  The freedom of the press in Ireland, 1784–1841, 20
Ingram, P.
  'Law and lawyers in Trollope's Ireland', 56n
Irish Law Reform Commission
  Offences against the Dublin police acts and related offences, 28
  Vagrancy and related offences, 28
The Irish Statutes revised edition: 3 Edward II to the Union, A.D. 1310–1800, 63n, 64
Irwin, L.
  'The Irish presidency courts, 1569–1672', 25

Jackson, C.
  'Irish political opposition to the passage of reform, 1883–98: the Criminal Evidence Act 1898', 49n
Jackson, John
  'Many years on in Northern Ireland: the Diplock legacy', 81
Jaconelli, J.
  'Human rights guarantees and Irish home rule', 41
Jaski, Bart
  'Marriage laws in Ireland and on the Continent in the early middle ages', 68
Johnson, D.S.
  'Cattle smuggling on the Irish border, 1932–38', 52n
  'The trials of Sam Gray: Monaghan politics and nineteenth-century Irish criminal procedure', 28, 49n
  'Trial by jury in Ireland, 1869–1914', 49n
Johnston, E.M.
  Great Britain and Ireland, 1760–1800: a study in political administration, 20, 31
Johnston-Liik, E.M.
  History of the Irish parliament 1692–1800: Commons, constituencies and statutes, 39
Jones, E.
  His life and times: the autobiography of the rt. hon. Sir Edward Jones, 61n

Kanter, Douglas
  'The Foxite Whigs, Irish legislative independence and the Act of Union, 1785–1806', 76
Kavanaugh, A.C.
  John Fitzgibbon, earl of Clare: protestant reaction and English authority in late eighteenth-century Ireland, 59

Keane, E., Phair, P.B., and Sadlier, T.U. (eds)
> *King's Inns admission papers, 1607–1867*, 32, 57–8, 91

Keane, R., 62
> 'The one judgment rule in the Supreme Court', 45
> 'The will of the general: martial law in Ireland 1535–1924', 41

Kearney, H.F.
> 'The court of wards and liveries in Ireland, 1622–1641', 24

Kelly, F.
> 'An Old-Irish text on court procedure', 67n
> *Audacht Moraind*, 67
> *Early Irish farming*, 66
> *A guide to early Irish law*, 66, 67

Kelly, James
> 'The abduction of women of fortune in eighteenth-century Ireland', 51
> *Gallows speeches from eighteenth-century Ireland*, 51
> 'Infanticide in eighteenth-century Ireland', 51n
> 'The making of law in eighteenth-century Ireland: the significance and import of Poynings' Law', 39n
> 'Monitoring the constitution: the operation of Poynings' Law in the 1760s', 39n
> 'A most inhuman and barbarous piece of villainy: an exploration of the crime of rape in eighteenth-century Ireland', 51, 53
> *Poynings' Law and the making of law in Ireland, 1660–1800*, 65
> *Prelude to Union: Anglo-Irish politics in the 1780s*, 39n
> 'The Privy Council of Ireland and the making of Irish law', 79
> 'Regulating print: the State and control of print in eighteenth-century Ireland', 75
> 'Scarcity and poor relief in eighteenth-century Ireland: the subsistence crisis of 1782–4', 42
> *That damn'd thing called honour: duelling in Ireland, 1570–1800*, 51

Kelly, J. (ed.)
> *The letters of Lord Chief Baron Edward Willes to the earl of Warwick, 1757–62: an account of Ireland in the mid-eighteenth century*, 59
> *Proceedings of the Irish House of Lords, 1771–1800*, 79

Kelly, Jennifer
> 'A study of Ribbonism in Co. Leitrim in 1841', 87n

Kelly, P.
> 'A disquisition touching that great question whether an act of parliament made in England shall bind the kingdom and people of Ireland without their allowance of such act in the kingdom of Ireland', 74–5
> 'Sir Richard Bolton and the authorship of "A declaration setting forth, and by what means, the laws and statutes of England, from time to time, came to be of force in Ireland,"' 74–5
> 'The Irish woollen export prohibition act of 1699: Kearney revisited', 21
> 'The printer's copy of the ms. of Molyneux's *The case of Ireland's being bound … (1698)*', 21
> 'William Molyneux and the spirit of liberty in eighteenth-century Ireland', 41

Kennedy, D.
> 'The Irish opposition, parliamentary reform and public opinion, 1792–1794', 40n

Kenny, Colum
    'Adventures in training: the Irish genesis of the remarkable and far-sighted Select Committee on Legal Education 1846', 56n
    '"By no means relished by the gentlemen of the bar": the King's Inns moves to Constitution Hill', 92
    'Counsellor Duhigg, antiquarian and activist', 63
    'The exclusion of Catholics from the legal profession in Ireland, 1537–1829', 57
    'The Four Courts in Dublin before 1796', 62
    'Irish ambition and English preference in chancery appointments, 1827–1841: the fate of William Conyngham Plunket', 60
    King's Inns and the battle of the books, 1972: cultural controversy at a Dublin library, 56
    King's Inns and the kingdom of Ireland: the Irish inn of court, 1541–1800, 55–6
    'On lawyers, their obligations and the Cicero collection at King's Inns Library', 91
    'The records of King's Inns', 56
    Tristram Kennedy and the revival of Irish legal training, 1835–1885, 56
Kent, Brad
    'The banning of George Bernard Shaw's *The adventures of the black girl in her search for God* and the decline of the Irish Academy of Letters', 77n
Kerr, D.A.
    Peel, priests and politics, 28
Kinealy, C.
    'A right to march? The conflict at Dolly's Brae', 41n
Kinsella, Eoin
    'In pursuit of a positive construction: Irish Catholics and the Williamite articles of surrender, 1690–1701', 75
Kissane, B.
    'Defending democracy? The legislative response to political extremism in the Irish Free State, 1922–39', 42n
Kleinrichert, D.
    Republican imprisonment and the prison ship Argenta, 55n
Knirck, Jason
    'The Dominion of Ireland: the Anglo-Irish Treaty in an Imperial context', 77
Knox, Alexander
    A history of the county of Down, 96
Kostel, R.W.
    'Rebels in the dock: the prosecution of the Dublin Fenians 1865–6', 51
Kotsonouris, M.
    Retreat from revolution: the Dáil courts, 1920–24, 44, 73
    The winding-up of the Dáil courts, 1922–1925: an obvious duty, 45, 73
Krause, T.
    'The influence of Sir Walter Crofton's Irish System on prison reform in Germany', 54

Laird, Heather
    Subversive law in Ireland, 1879–1920: from unwritten law to the Dáil courts, 44n

Lammey, D.
'The growth of the patriot opposition in Ireland during the 1770s', 40n
Lamoine, G. (ed.)
'Charges to the grand jury', 60n
Langan, P.S.J.
'Irish material from the state trials', 23
Lapoint, E.C.
'Irish immunity to witch-hunting 1534–1711', 51
Larkin, F.M.
'Judge Bodkin and the 1916 Rising: a letter to his son', 61
Larkin, F.M., and Dawson, N. (eds)
Lawyers, the law and history, 58n, 73n, 77n, 80n, 89n, 90n, 91n, 92n
Larkin, J.F.
'John Blake Powell (1861–1923), judge', 31
Lowe, W.J.
'Policing famine Ireland', 53
'The constabulary agitation of 1882', 54
'The war against the RIC, 1919–21', 54
Lowry, Lord
'The Irish lords of appeal in ordinary', 61n
Luddy, M.
'A sinister and retrogressive proposal: Irish women's opposition to the 1937 draft Constitution', 41
Luddy, Maria
Prostitution and Irish society, 88n
Lyall, A.
'The Irish House of Lords as a judicial body, 1783–1800', 43
Lyall, A. (ed.)
Irish Exchequer Reports, 1716–34, 80, 89, 93–4
Lyons, M.C.
Illustrated incumbered estates: Ireland, 1850–1905 – lithographic and other illustrative material in the incumbered estates rentals, 44n
Lysaght, C.E.
'The Irish peers and the House of Lords', 22

McCabe, D.
'Magistrates, peasants and the petty session courts, Mayo, 1823–50', 44n
'Open court: law and the expansion of magisterial jurisdiction at petty sessions in nineteenth-century Ireland', 44n
McCafferty, J.
'To follow the late precedents of England: the Irish impeachment proceedings of 1641', 38
McCarthy, John-Paul
'"In hope and fear": the Victorian prison in perspective', 88
McCavitt, J.
'Good planets in their several spheares: the establishment of the assize circuits in early seventeenth-century Ireland', 36n
McColgan, J.
British policy and the Irish administration, 1920–22, 20

McCone, Kim, and Simms, Katharine (eds)
  Progress in medieval Irish studies, 67
McCormack, A.M.
  The earldom of Desmond, 1463–1583: the decline and crisis of a feudal lordship, 71
McCormack, W.J.
  Introduction to *The Parliamentary Register of Ireland, 1781–1797*, 64, 78n
  'Vision and revision in the study of eighteenth century Irish parliament rhetoric', 40n
McCracken, D.P.
  Inspector Mallon: buying Irish patriotism for a five-pound note, 88
McCullough, Niall
  Introduction to *The courthouses of Ireland: a gazetteer*, 62
MacDermott, J.C.
  An enriching life, 61n
MacDonagh, O.
  The inspector general: Sir Jeremiah Fitzpatrick and the politics of social reform, 1783–1802, 29
  'The last bill of pains and penalties: the case of Daniel O'Sullivan 1869', 27
McDonnell, A.D.
  The life of Sir Denis Henry Catholic Unionist, 61n
McDowell, R.B.
  Ireland in the age of imperialism and revolution, 1760–1801, 18–19, 20, 39n
  The Irish administration, 1801–1914, 18, 24, 29
  The Irish convention, 1917–1918, 20, 21
McEldowney, J.F.
  'The case of *The Queen v. McKenna* (1869) and jury packing in Ireland', 28
  'Challenges in legal bibliography: the role of biography in legal history', 63
  'Dicey and the sovereignty of parliament: lessons from Irish legal history', 63n
  'Paul O'Higgins (1927–2008)', 92
  'Thomas O'Hagan (1812–85), judge', 30
McElligott, A., Chambers, L., Breathnach, C., and Lawless, C. (eds)
  Power in history from medieval Ireland to the post-modern world, 76n
McFeely, M.D.
  Lady inspectors: the campaign for a better workplace, 1893–1921, 48
McGrath, Brid
  'Ireland and the third university: attendance at the Inns of Court, 1603–1649', 90–1
McGrath, C.I.
  'Central aspects of the eighteenth century constitutional framework in Ireland: the Government Supply Bill and Biennial Parliamentary Sessions 1715–82', 39n
  'Government, parliament and the constitution: the reinterpretation of Poynings' Law, 1692–1714', 75
  The making of the eighteenth-century Irish constitution: government, parliament and the revenue 1692–1714, 39
  'Securing the Protestant interest: the origins and purpose of the penal laws of 1695', 40
  'The "Union" representation of 1703 in the Irish House of Commons: a case of mistaken identity', 75n

McGrath, Claire
   'The Anglo-Irish treaty, 1921: myths and strategies', 76
McGuire, J.
   'A lawyer in politics: the career of Sir Richard Nagle, c.1636–1699', 57
McIvor, F.J. (ed.)
   Elegantia juris: selected writings of F.H. Newark, 14
McKenna, John (ed.)
   A beleagured station: the memoir of Head Constable John McKenna, 1891–1921, 88
MacLean, Heather, Gentles, Ian, and Ó Siochrú, Micheál
   'Minutes of court martial held in Dublin in the years 1651–3 [with index]', 80
McLeod, Neil
   Early Irish contract law, 66
MacLysaght, E.
   Irish life in the seventeenth century, 30n
McMahon, D.
   'The chief justice and the governor general controversy in 1932', 22
McMahon, Michael
   The murder of Thomas Douglas Bateson, Monaghan, 1851, 87n
McMahon, R.
   'The court of petty sessions and the law in pre-Famine Galway', 44n
   '"The fear of the vengeance": the prosecution of homicide in pre-Famine and Famine Ireland', 85
   '"Let the law take its course": punishment and the exercise of the prerogative of mercy in pre-Famine and Famine Ireland', 86
   'Manor courts in the west of Ireland before the Famine', 44
   '"A violent society"? Homicide rates in Ireland, 1831–1850', 86
McMahon, Richard (ed.)
   Crime, law and popular culture in Europe, 1500–1900, 85
McManus, Damian
   'Niall Frosach's "Act of truth": a bardic apologue in a poem for Sir Nicholas Walsh, Chief Justice of the Common Pleas (1615)', 89
Macmillan, G.
   'British subjects and Irish citizens: the passport controversy 1923–24', 41
McNally, P.
   Parties, patriots and undertakers, 40n
MacNiocaill, G.
   'The contact of Irish and common law', 36n
   'The interaction of laws', 16, 36n
McParland, E.
   'The early history of James Gandon's Four Courts', 62
   'The old Four Courts at Christ Church', 62
Maddox, N.P.
   'A melancholy record: the story of the nineteenth-century Irish Party Processions Act', 41
Magennis, E.
   The Irish political system, 1740–1765: the golden age of undertakers, 40n
Magennis, E.F.
   'A Presbyterian insurrection? Reconsidering the Hearts of Oak disturbances of July 1763', 52n

Maguire, C.
  'The Republican courts', 44n
Maitland, F.W.
  Letters, 103
Malcolm, E.
  The Irish policeman, 1822–1922: a life, 53
  'The reign of terror in Carlow: the politics of policing in Ireland in the late 1830s', 52n
  'Troops of largely diseased women: VD, the Contagious Diseases Acts and moral policing in the late nineteenth-century Ireland', 51–2
Malcomson, A.P.W.
  'The Irish peerage and the Union, 1800–1971', 40
  The pursuit of the heiress: aristocratic marriage in Ireland, 1750–1820, 51n
  Virtues of a wicked earl: the life and legend of William Sydney Clements, 3rd earl of Leitrim, 1806–78, 87
Malcomson, A.P.W., and Jackson, D.J.
  'Sir Henry Cavendish and proceedings of the Irish House of Commons, 1776–1800', 64n
Mansergh, N.
  'The Government of Ireland Act 1920: its origins and purpose', 21
Marshall, R.D.
  'Lieutenant W.E. Wylie, KC: the soldiering lawyer of 1716', 89
Martin, John A.H.
  'Reflections on judicial dress with particular reference to the county and circuit courts', 90
Martin, Peter
  Censorship in the two Irelands, 1922–1939, 77
Maynard, Hazel
  'The Irish legal profession and the Catholic revival, 1660–89', 91
Mercer, Malcolm
  'Select document: Exchequer malpractice in late medieval Ireland: a petition from Christopher Fleming, Lord Slane, 1438', 69
Milne, Kenneth
  The Dublin Liberties, 1600–1850, 80
Milsom, S.F.C.
  review of G.R. Elton's *F.W. Maitland*, 33n
Mohr, Thomas, 90
  'Brehon law before twentieth century courts', 67n
  'A British Empire court: a brief appraisal of the history of the Judicial Committee of the Privy Council', 76n
  'British imperial statutes and Irish sovereignty: statutes passed after the creation of the Irish Free State', 77n
  'British involvement in the creation of the Constitution of the Irish Free State', 77
  'The Colonial Laws Validity Act and the Irish Free State', 77
  'The foundations of Irish extra-territorial legislation', 77
  'Law in Gaelic Utopia: perceptions of brehon law in nineteenth- and early twentieth-century Ireland', 67n

'Law without loyalty – the abolition of the Irish appeal to the privy council', 45, 76
'The rights of women under the Constitution of the Irish Free State', 78
'Salmon of knowledge', 45n
Molyneux, William
    The case of Ireland's ... stated, 64, 74
Moore, David
    'From potatoes and peasants to quotas and squires: the endurability of conacre from 1845 to 1995', 47
Moran, G.
    'Philip Callan: the rise and fall of an Irish nationalist MP, 1868–1885', 58
Morgan, H.
    'Extradition and treason-trial of a Gaelic lord: the case of Brian O'Rourke', 50–1
Morgan, H. (ed.)
    Political ideology in Ireland, 1541–1641, 38n
Mori, Setsuko
    'Irish monasticism and the concept of inheritance: an examination of its legal aspects', 68
Mullaney, Susan
    'The 1791 Irish Apothecary's Act: the first nationwide regulation of apothecaries in the British Isles', 79n
Murphy, B.
    'The lawyer as historian: *Magna Carta* and the public right of fishery', 33
Murphy, J.A., and Murphy, Clíona
    'Burials and bigotry in early nineteenth-century Ireland', 76

Newark, F.H.
    'Notes on Irish legal history', 14, 24, 33
Ní Chatháin, Próinséas, and Richter, Michael (eds)
    Irland und die Christenheit: Bibelstudien und Mission / Ireland and Christendom: the Bible and the missions, 67
Ní Dhonnchadha, Máirín
    'The Lex innocentium: Adoman's law for women, clerics and youths, 697 A.D.', 67
Ní Mhunghaile, Lesa
    'The legal system in Ireland and the Irish language, 1700–*c*.1843', 72
Ní Mhurchadha, Maighréad
    'Documents concerning the oath of supremacy in early seventeenth-century Ireland', 71
Nicholls, K.
    'A calendar of salved Chancery pleadings concerning County Louth', 43
    Gaelic and Gaelicized Ireland in the middle ages, 16
    The O Doyne (Ó Duinn) Manuscript, 16, 36n
    'Some documents on Irish law and custom in the sixteenth century', 16
Nowlan, A.J.
    'Kilmainham jail', 29

O'Brien, G.
    Anglo-Irish politics in the age of Grattan and Pitt, 39n

'Capital punishment in Ireland, 1922–1964', 55n
'The missing personnel records of the RIC', 54
'The new Poor Law in pre-Famine Ireland: a case history', 42
Ó Broin, L.
    W.E. Wylie and the Irish revolution, 1916–1921, 61
Ó Brudair, Dáibhí
    Duanaire Dháibhidh Uí Bhruadair, 89n
O'Byrne, Eileen (ed.)
    The Convert Rolls: The Calendar of the Convert Rolls, 1703–1838 with Fr. Wallace Clare's annotated list of converts, 1703–78, 75
O'Carroll, G.
    Robert Day (1746–1841): the diaries and addresses to the grand juries, 1793–1829, 60
Ó Cathasaigh, Tomas
    review of *A companion to the Corpus Iuris Hibernici*, 66
Ó Cearúil, Micheál
    Bunreacht na hEireann: a study of the Irish text, 77n
O'Connell, M.R. (ed.)
    The correspondence of Daniel O'Connell, 32
O'Connor, E.
    'Active sabotage in industrial conflict, 1817–23', 48
    A labour history of Ireland, 1824–1960, 48
Ó Corráin, Donnchadh
    'Some legal references to fences and fencing in early historic Ireland', 68
Ó Corráin, Donnchadh, Breatnach, Liam, and McCone, Kim (eds)
    Sages, saints and storytellers: Celtic studies in honour of Professor James Carney, 67
Ó Cróinín, Dáibhí
    Early medieval Ireland, 400–1200, 66, 67
Ó Cróinín, Dáibhí (ed.)
    A new history of Ireland: i – prehistoric and early Ireland, 66n, 67
O'Donnell, I.
    'Lethal violence in Ireland, 1841 to 2003', 55n
O'Donnell, I., and McAuley, F. (eds)
    Criminal justice history: themes and controversies from pre-independence Ireland, 53, 54
O'Donoghue, Aoife
    'The inimitable form of Irish neutrality: from the birth of the State to World War II', 77–8
O'Dowd, M.
    'Women and the Irish chancery court in the late sixteenth and early seventeenth centuries', 43
O'Dowd, M. (ed.)
    Calendar of State Papers, Ireland: Tudor period, 1571–1575, 64
O'Flaherty, E.
    'Ecclesiastical politics and the dismantling of the penal laws in Ireland', 40
    'Urban politics and municipal reform in Limerick, 1723–62', 42n
O'Flanagan, P., Ferguson, P., and Whelan, K. (eds)
    Rural Ireland, 1600–1900: modernisation and change, 82

O'Grady, J.P.
   'The Irish Free State passport and the question of Irish citizenship 1921–4',
      41
O'Hanrahan, M.
   'The tithe war in Co. Kilkenny 1830–34', 52n
O'Higgins, P.
   'Arthur Browne (1756–1805), civilian', 30
   A bibliography of Irish trials and other legal proceedings, 32, 62
   A bibliography of periodical literature relating to Irish law, 32–3
   'Blasphemy in Irish law', 28
   'An essay on puzzles in Irish legal bibliography', 62, 63n
   'William Ridgeway (1765–1817), law reporter', 30
   'William Sampson (1764–1836), emigrant lawyer', 30
   '*Wright v Fitzgerald* revisited', 23
O'Higgins, T.F.
   A double life, 61n
Ohlmeyer, J., 49
   'Irish recusant lawyers during the reign of Charles I', 57, 90
   'Records of the Irish court of Chancery: a preliminary report for 1627 to 1634',
      43
Ohlmeyer, J. (ed.)
   Political thought in seventeenth-century Ireland, 38n
Ohlmeyer, J., and Ó'Ciardha, E. (eds)
   The Irish statute staple books, 1596–1687, 49
Ó hÓgartaigh, Margaret
   'Antonia MacDonnell, Meath's first female barrister and the legal profession
      in the early twentieth century', 92
   'Female teachers and professional trade unions in early twentieth-century
      Ireland', 84
Ollerenshaw, P.
   The Belfast banks, 1825–1914, 49
Ó Longaigh, S.
   Emergency law in independent Ireland, 1922–48, 38n
Ó Maitiú, S.
   The humours of Donnybrook: Dublin's famous fair and its suppression, 53n
O'Malley, L.
   'Law', 92–3
   'Patrick Darcy – Galway lawyer and politician 1598–1668', 57
Ó Muirí, R.
   'The burning of Wildgoose Lodge', 52n
O'Neill, M.S.
   'In time of "war": Irish domestic security legislation 1939–45', 81n
O'Reilly, Stan J.
   'Tales from Wicklow Gaol: murder, confinement and escape', 87
Osborough, W.N., 27, 32
   '6 Anne, chapter 19: "setting and preserving a public library for ever"', 79
   'Another country, other days: revisiting Thomas Kilroy's *The big chapel*', 46, 84
   'Bishop Dixon, the Irish historian and Irish law', 64n

Borstal in Ireland: custodial provision for the young adult offender, 1906–1974, 29
'Chapters from the history of the dramatic author's performing right', 84
'Constitutionally constructing a sense of oneness: facets of law in Ireland after the Union', 41n
'The Dublin Castle career (1866–78) of Bram Stoker', 90
'Early eighteenth-century charitable relief for two fire-damaged Ulster towns', 85
'Ecclesiastical law and the Reformation in Ireland', 43
'Extramural pursuits of the eighteenth-century bench', 60
'The failure to enact an Irish bill of rights: a gap in Irish constitutional history', 41
'Forcibly commandeered transport and owner's insurance: the deciding of two test cases in the 1920s', 19, 49
'The history of Irish legal publishing: a challenge unmet', 62
'In search of Irish legal history: a gap for explorers', 95
'The Irish custom of tracts', 36n
'Irish law and the rights of the national school-teacher', 28
'The Irish legal system, 1796–1877', 37
'Landmarks in the history of King's Inns', 58
Law and the emergence of modern Dublin: a litigation topography for a capital city, 65n, 76n
'Law in Ireland, 1916–1926', 19, 37
'Legal aspects of the 1798 rising, its suppression and the aftermath', 37n
'Legal history: confronting the challenge', 94
'The legislation of the pre-Union Irish parliament', 63n
'The legislative deficit in eighteenth-century Ireland', 79
'Murder or manslaughter: a 1739 decision of the Irish King's Bench', 51
'Mysteries and solutions: experiencing Irish legal history', 64n
'An outline history of the penal system in Ireland', 29
'Publishing the law: John Finlay (1780–1856)', 63
'Puzzles from Irish law reporting history', 63
'Recollection of things past – trams, their clientele and the law', 48n
'Roman law in Ireland', 48n
'Scholarship and the university law school', 34
'Some nineteenth-century Irish litigation over commons and enclosures', 82
Studies in Irish legal history, 36n, 61, 63n
'The title of the last lord chief justice of Ireland', 61
'Tribulations of a king's printer: George Grierson II in court', 63
'The [U.C.D.] law school's early professoriate', 93
'Wills that go missing: the quest for the last testament of Christopher Wandesford, lord deputy of Ireland, 1640', 45
Osborough, W.N., and Hogan, D. (eds)
  Brehons and attorneys: studies in the history of the Irish legal profession, 102
Ó Siochrú, M.
  Confederate Ireland, 1642–1649: a constitutional and political analysis, 37n
O'Sullivan, D.J.
  The Irish constabularies, 1822–1922: a century of policing in Ireland, 53
O'Sullivan, Eoin, and O'Donnell, Ian
  Coercive confinement in Ireland: patients, prisoners and penitents, 88
Oxford dictionary of national biography, 59, 89

Palmer, S.H.
> *Police and protest in England and Ireland, 1780–1850*, 54
> 'The Irish police experiment; the beginnings of modern police in the British Isles, 1785–95', 53

Park, P.
> 'The combination acts in Ireland, 1727–1825', 28

The Parliamentary Register of Ireland, 1781–1797, 64, 73n, 78, 78n

Paterson, T.G.F.
> 'The Armagh manor court rolls', 27
> 'The burning of Wildgoose Lodge', 52n

Patterson, James G.
> 'Republicanism, agrarianism and banditry in the west of Ireland, 1798–1803', 87

Patterson, N.T.
> 'Brehon law in the late middle ages: "antiquarian and obsolete" or "traditional and functional"?', 36n, 67
> *Early Irish kinship: the legal structure of the agnatic descent group*, 69
> 'Gaelic law and the Tudor conquest of Ireland: the social background of the sixteenth-century recensions of the pseudo-historical prologue to the Senchas Már', 36, 67
> 'Patrilineal groups in early Irish society: the evidence from the Irish law texts', 69n

Pawlisch, H.S.
> *Sir John Davies and the conquest of Ireland: a study in legal imperialism*, 16, 30, 36
> 'Sir John Davies' law reports and the case of proxies', 16, 45

Phillips, Seymour
> 'David MacCarwell and the proposal to purchase English law, *c*.1273–*c*.1280', 69

Pole, Adam
> 'Role of the sheriff in Victorian Ireland', 73
> 'Sheriffs' sales during the land war', 1879–82', 73

Poppe, Erich
> 'The genealogy of Émin(e) in the Book of Leinster', 67
> 'A new edition of Cáin Éimíne Báin', 67

Powell, Martyn
> 'Ireland's urban houghers; moral economy and popular protest in the late eighteenth century', 87

Power, A.
> 'The eighteenth-century origins of the Irish doctrine of graft', 47

Power, P.C.
> *The courts martial of 1798–9*, 37n

Power, T.
> 'The Black Book of King's Inns: an introduction with an abstract of contents', 32, 58n
> 'Conversions among the legal profession in Ireland in the eighteenth century', 57

Power, T.P., and Whelan, K. (eds)
> *Endurance and emergence: Catholics in Ireland in the eighteenth century*, 40

Price, Huw
> 'Early Irish canons and medieval Welsh law', 68n

Prior, P., and Griffiths, D.
　'The chaplaincy question – The lord lieutenant v. The Belfast lunatic asylum', 46n
Quigley, W.G.H., and Roberts, E.F.D. (eds)
　Registrum Iohannis Mey: the register of John Mey, archbishop of Armagh, 1443–1456, 70
Quinn, A.P.
　Wigs and guns: Irish barristers in the Great War, 58n
Quinn, D.B.
　'The early interpretation of Poynings' Law: part I, 1494–1615', 39n
　'Government printing and the publication of the Irish statutes in the sixteenth century', 32n

Redmond, L.
　'Irish appeals to the House of Lords in the eighteenth century', 24
Redmond, Mary
　'The emergence of women in the solicitors' profession in Ireland', 56–7
Reece, B.
　The origins of Irish convict transportation to New South Wales, 54
Reidy, Conor
　Ireland's 'moral hospital': the Irish borstal system, 1906–1956, 88
Richardson, Caleb
　'"They are not worthy of themselves": *The Tailor and Ansty* debates of 1942', 77n
Robins, J.
　Fools and mad: a history of the insane in Ireland, 46n
　The lost children: a study of charity children in Ireland, 1700–1900, 29
Rock, Suzanne
　'The impact of the Stamp Act crisis, 1765–6 in Ireland', 75
Rockett, Kevin
　Irish film censorship: a cultural journey from silent cinema to internet pornography, 77
Rogan, Mary
　'The Prison Rules, 1947: political imprisonment, politics and legislative change in Ireland', 88
Ryan, Louise, and Ward, Margaret (eds)
　Irish women and the vote: becoming citizens, 78
Ryan-Smolin, W.
　King's Inns portraits, 56

Shepard, Christopher
　'A liberalisation of Irish social policy? Women's organisations and the campaign for women police in Ireland, 1915–57', 88
Simms, J.G.
　'The bishops' banishment act of 1697', 20
　Jacobite Ireland, 1685–91, 20
　'The making of a penal law, 1703–4', 20
　The Williamite confiscation in Ireland, 1690–1703, 27
Simms, K.
　'The legal position of Irishwomen in the later middle ages', 28

Simpson, A.W. (ed.)
  Biographical dictionary of the common law, 31
Sinclair, Georgina
  'The "Irish" policeman and the Empire: influencing the policing of the British Empire/Commonwealth', 88n
Smith, B.A.
  'The Irish general prisons board, 1877–1885: efficient deterrence or bureaucratic ineptitude?', 29
  'The Irish prison system, 1885–1914: land war to world war', 29
Smith, Brendan (ed.)
  The register of Milo Sweteman, archbishop of Armagh, 1361–1380, 70
  The register of Nicholas Fleming, archbishop of Armagh, 1404–1416, 70
Smith, Jeremy
  'Federalism, devolution and partition: Sir Edward Carson and the search for a compromise on the Third Home Rule Bill, 1913–14', 76
Stacey, R.C.
  The road to judgment: from custom to court in medieval Ireland and Wales, 66–7
  'Ties that bind: immunities in Celtic law', 69
Sughi, M.A.
  'The appointment of Octavian de Palatio as archbishop of Armagh, 1477–8', 46n
Sughi, M.A. (ed.)
  Registrum Octaviani: the register of Octavian de Palatio, archbishop of Armagh, 1478–1513, 46, 70
Sullivan, F.S.
  Lectures on the constitution and laws of England with a commentary on Magna Carta, etc., 64
Sweeney, Frank
  The murder of Conell Boyle, County Donegal, 1898, 87
Sweeney, J.C.
  'Admiralty law of Arthur Browne', 63

Tallon, G.
  Court of Claims: submissions and evidence, 1663, 65n
Towey, J.
  'Hugh Kennedy and the constitutional development of the Irish Free State 1922–23', 22
Townsend, C.
  Political violence in Ireland: government resistance since 1848, 52–3
Treadwell, V.
  'The Irish court of wards under James I', 24
Treadwell, V. (ed.)
  The Irish Commission of 1622: an investigation of the Irish Administration, 1615–1622, and its consequences, 65n
Turvey, Roger
  The treason and trial of Sir John Perrot, 86
Tyrrell, Peter
  Founded on fear: Letterfrack Industrial School, war and exile, 88

Vaughan, W.E.
Landlords and tenants in mid-Victorian Ireland, 46
Murder trials in Ireland, 1836–1914, 73, 85
Sin, sheep and Scotsmen: John George Adair and the Derryveagh evictions, 1861, 46n

Veach, Colm T.
'Henry II's grant of Meath to Hugh de Lacy in 1172', 69

Vesey, Padraig
The murder of Major Mahon, Strokestown, Co. Roscommon, 1847, 87

Victory, I.
'The making of the declaratory act of 1720', 39n

Wall, M.
Catholic Ireland in the eighteenth century, collected essays, 40
The penal laws, 1691–1760, 18

Windrum, C.
'The provision and practice of prison reform in County Down', 55n

Wolf, J.B.
'Withholding their due: the dispute between Ireland and Great Britain over unemployment insurance payments to conditionally landed Irish wartime volunteer workers', 49n

Wood, H., 94
'The court of castle chamber or star chamber of Ireland', 25n, 42
'The destruction of the Public Records', 94
A Guide to the records deposited in the Public Record Office of Ireland, 14, 24, 25, 94

Wylie, J.C.W.
'The Irishness of Irish land law', 47

Yager, T.
'Mass eviction in the Mullet peninsula during and after the Great Famine', 47

Yale, D.E.C.
'Notes on the jurisdiction of the admiralty in Ireland', 26

General index

abuse of power, 38
Act of Union, 1800, 19, 20, 23, 39, 40n, 56, 63, 65, 76, 79
administration of justice *see* criminal justice
administrative law, 29–30
admiralty court, 26, 30, 43, 60, 81
admiralty law, 63
Adomnan's law, 67n
The adventures of the black girl in her search for God (Shaw), 77n
agrarian unrest, 25, 30, 52, 87
Alexander, Jerome, 91
Anglo-Hibernian constitution, 41
Anglo-Irish Treaty, 1921, 21, 44, 76, 77n
apothecaries, 79n
appeals, 24, 43, 45, 76
Archer-Shee case, 58, 92n
archives, 13, 85, 94–5 *see also* Four Courts
Argenta (prison ship), 55
Armagh, 27, 93
   archiepiscopal registers, 46, 69–70, 97
Arthur Cox Foundation, 63
assizes, 36, 71, 72, 86n
Aston, Richard, 60
Atkinson, Lord, 60
attorney general, office of, 22
attorneys *see* solicitors
Austen, Jane, 100
Australia, 54

Bagwell, Richard, 13
banking, 49
bardic eulogies, 89–90
barristers, 31–2, 56, 58, 92 *see also* King's Inns; legal profession

Bateson, Thomas Douglas, 87n
Behan, Brendan, 42
Belfast, 49n, 53, 88
Berry, H.F., 13
Betham, William, 99
Bettesworth, Serjeant, 89
bibliography, 32–3, 62–3, 67
The big chapel (Kilroy), 84
Bill of Rights, 41
biography, 30–1, 59–61, 89
Black Book of King's Inns, 32, 58n
blasphemy, 28
Bodkin, Matthias, judge, 61
Bolingbroke, Henry St John, 26
Bolton, Sir Richard, 38, 74
Book of Leinster, 67n
borough courts, 27
borstals, 29, 87–8
boundary commission, 21
Boyce, Eamonn, 88n
Boyle, Conell, 87n
Bramhall, John, bishop, 38
Bray, Co. Wicklow, 82n
brehon law, 16, 36–7, 66–9, 99
British Commonwealth, 77, 88
British Empire, 77, 88
British national parks, 82
Brouncker, Sir Henry, 71
Browne, Arthur, 30, 63
burials, 76

Cahermacnaghten, Co. Clare, 66n
Cairns, Hugh McCalmont, 31
Calendars of Justiciary Rolls, 97
Callaghan, Cornelius, 89
Callan, Co. Kilkenny, 46, 84
Callan, Philip, 58
Camden Society, 60, 64
canals, 29

133

capital punishment, 55
Carlow, county, 52
Carney, James, 67
Carrigan Committee, 1930–31, 77n
Carson, Edward, 58, 60, 76n, 92n
Carver, Martin, 97
Casement, Sir Roger, 86
Casey v. Irish Sailors' and Soldiers' Land Trust (1937), 83
Castle Chamber, court of, 24–5, 42–3
Catholic Church, 46, 78
Catholic emancipation, 23, 31
Catholics, 28, 39n, 40, 46, 57, 61n, 75n, 88n, 89, 91 *see also* penal laws
cattle smuggling, 52
censorship, 75, 77
certiorari, 86
cess, 38
'chamber counsel' lawyers, 91
chancery, court of, 24, 36, 43, 44, 60, 60n, 80
charities law, 27–8, 85
Charles I, king, 38, 42, 57, 90
Charles II, king, 37 *see also* Restoration
Cherry, R.R., 60
chief herald, office of, 76
Christ Church, Dublin, 69n, 80
Christian, Jonathan, 32, 60
chronological surveys, 15–19
church, 17–18, 23, 46, 68, 85 *see also* Catholic Church; Church of Ireland; ecclesiastical courts; ecclesiastical law; penal laws
church briefs, 85
Church of England Record Society, 70
Church of Ireland, 25, 76, 79, 91
Cicero, 91
circuit courts, 90n
civil bill, 49
civil liability, 83–4
civil procedure, 49
civil war, 1922–23, 14, 55
Claims, court of, 65n
Clare, Fr Wallace, 75
Cleary, Bridget, 51
Clements, William Sydney, 3rd earl of Leitrim, 87

Clonmel, Co. Tipperary, 87–8
Clonmell, earl of, 72
Clonshire, Co. Limerick, 71
coercive confinement, 88
Coghill, Marmaduke, 59–60
Colonial Laws Validity Act, 77
Columbia University, New York, 93
combination acts, 28
commercial law, 49, 84
common law, 36–7, 69, 89
common law courts, 15, 17, 18, 23–5, 30, 99
common pleas, court of, 23, 79, 89
commons, 82
Comyn inheritance, 69
conacre, 47
conciliar jurisdiction, 15, 24
Confederation of Kilkenny, 37
Congested Districts Board, 78
Connacht presidency, 25, 71
conscience, court of, 27
Constitution of 1937, 41–2, 77
Constitution of the Irish Free State, 1922, 22, 31, 77, 78
Constitutional Court, 90
constitutional history, 17, 19–27, 37, 38–42, 74–8
Contagious Diseases Acts, 52
contract law, 66
convert rolls, 75
conveyancing, 19
Convict Reference Files (National Archives), 85
convict system, 29, 54
convocations, records of, 70
Conyngham, Col. William Burton, 93
Cook, John, 30
Cork, county, 87
corruption, 69
Costello, Declan, judge, 102
Cotter, James, 50
Council of the Marches (Wales), 72
Council of the North, 71–2
county courts, 90n
courthouses, 62, 93
courts, 15, 17, 18, 19, 23–7, 30, 36, 42–3, 44, 79–81, 99 *see also* admiralty court; ecclesiastical

courts; judiciary; law reporting; trials
courts-martial, 80
Craig-Collins pact, 1922, 22
Cregan, Donal, 90
crime, 50, 51–3, 55
criminal damage to property, 28
criminal evidence, 49
criminal justice, 28, 48, 50–5, 85–8
criminal procedure, 22, 28, 49, 86
criminal trials, 85–7
Crofton, Sir Walter, 29, 54
Cromer, George, archbishop of Armagh, 70
Cromwell, Oliver, 37
Cromwellian period, 24, 30, 37
Crow Street Theatre, Dublin, 72
Crown Cases Reserved, court for, 44
Crown courts, 44, 74
Crumlin manor court, 26
cultural nationalism, 34
Curragh of Kildare, 82–3

Dáil courts, 19, 38n, 44–5, 73
Dáil Éireann, 19, 99
Dalkey, Co. Dublin, 82n
Daly, Richard, 72
Darcy, Patrick, 17, 57
Davies, Sir John, 16, 30, 36, 45, 80, 94
Dawson, Norma
    tribute to Osborough (2011), 101–4
Day, Robert, 60
de Lacy, Hugh, 69
de Palatio, Octavian, 46, 70
de Valera, Eamon, 22
Dease, E.J.C., 61
Deasy's Act, 47
debt, law of, 18
Decrees of Dáil Éireann, 1919–22, 99
defamation law, 46, 72–3
Delvin, Co. Westmeath, 83–4
Desmond, earldom of, 71
Desmond palatinate (Kerry), 71
Dicey, C.V., 63n
Diplock courts, 81n
discrimination, 18
Domville, Sir William, 74
Donegal, county, 46, 48, 87

'Donegan' affair, 22
Donnybrook Fair, 53
Dove, P.E., 103
Down, county, 55, 96
Downing, John, 71, 86
dramatic author's performing right, 84
Dublin, 26, 27, 65, 72, 76n, 79, 84 *see also* Four Courts; King's Inns
    courts-martial (1651–1653), 80
    liberties, 80
    local courts, 80–1
    police acts, 28
    police strike (1882), 54n
    special juries, 73
    tolls and duties, 81
Dublin Castle, 30, 76, 90n
Dublin Corporation, 81n
Dublin Fenians, 51
Dublin Institute for Advanced Studies, 66
Dublin Law Institute, 56
Dublin Metropolitan Police, 53, 54
Dublin Record Office, Four Courts, 94
Duffy, George Gavan, 30
Duhigg, Bartholomew, 63, 99
Dun, John, 97
Dunlop, Robert, 13
Dunluce manor court, 26
Dursey Island, Co. Cork, 71

early Irish law, 16, 17, 36–7, 66–9, 99
early medieval period, 66–8
Easement of Burials Act, 1825, 76
Eastenders (BBC), 97
Easter Rising courts-martial, 41
ecclesiastical courts, 25, 43
ecclesiastical law, 43, 45–6, 68
ecclesiastical politics, 79
education, 78 *see also* legal education
Egan v. Macready (1921), 23
Eighteenth-Century Ireland, 35
Éire-Ireland, 35
electoral franchise, 41, 78
Elizabethan period, 16, 38, 42, 43, 51, 74, 86
Emmet, Robert, 86

employers' liability, 48
enclosures, 82
England, 15, 24, 36, 50, 60, 71–2, 96, 97
English Inns of Court *see* London Inns
English law, 47, 69
Enniskillen, Co. Fermanagh, 85
equity, courts of, 25
Esker manor court, 26
evangelical Protestantism, 53
evictions, 82n
exchequer, court of, 23, 24, 69, 80, 86, 93–4, 99
Exclusion Crisis, 1679–81, 75n
execution, sentence of, 85
extra-territorial legislation, 77

Factories Acts, 1679–81, 48
Faculty of Advocates (Scotland), 56
Falkiner, C.L., 13
family law, 28
Famine period, 85n
Farrell, Paul, 50
fences, 68
Fenians, 51
Fenton, Sir Geoffrey, 74
Ferguson, James, 99–100
feudal period, 24, 69
fiat, 72–3
film censorship, 77
Finlay, John, 63
Finlay, T.A., 96
First World War, 58, 76, 83
fishery, right of, 33
Fitzgerald, David, 75n
Fitzgerald, Lord, 60
Fitzgibbon, John, earl of Clare, 59
Fitzpatrick, Hugh, 62, 63
Fitzpatrick, Sir Jeremiah, 29
Flanagan, J.W., 61
Fleming, Christopher, lord of Slane, 69
Fleming, Nicholas, archbishop of Armagh, 46, 69, 70
flight of the earls, 16
folk tradition, 65
Four Courts, Dublin, 62, 93
    destruction of public records, 1922, 23–4, 62, 94, 100

Four Courts Press, 102
Franks family, 87n
Froude, J.A., 13

Gaelic kinship, 68, 69
Gaelic law *see* brehon law
Gaelic society, 14, 15, 16, 36, 68n
gallows speeches, 51
Gandon, James, 62, 93
gaol deliveries, 72
gavelkind, 36
George, Denis, 60
George III, king, 37
Georgian period, 73
Germany, 54
Gifford v. Loftus, 17
Gilbert, John, 13, 99
Government of Ireland Act, 1920, 21
government printing, 32n
governor-general controversy (1932), 22
graft, doctrine of, 47
Graham, E., 22n
Grattan's parliament, 21, 26
Greer, Desmond, 101, 103
Grierson, George II, 63
Guy Mannering (Scott), 98

habeas corpus, 23, 41
Hanna v. Irish Sailors' and Soldiers' Land Trust (1936), 83
Hansard, 78
Harley, Robert, 72
Harrington v. Crowley (1945), 83
Hart, Tony, 102
Healy, T.M., 58
Hearne, John, 90n
'Hearts of Oak' disturbances, 52
Henry, Sir Denis, 61
Henry II, king, 69
Henry VIII, king, 55
Hertford Irish estates, 47
Heuston, Robert, 92
high commission, 25
Historical Manuscripts Commission, 43
Hogan, Daire, 102
Holdsworth, Sir W.S., 14

General index

Home Rule, 41, 76
homicide, 85–6, 87, 88n
House of Commons, 72–3
House of Lords, 18, 22, 24, 40, 61 see also Irish House of Lords
  Irish judicial appointments, 60–1
housing, of First World War ex-servicemen, 76, 83
Howard, Gorges Edmond, 89
human rights, 41
Hunter v. Coleman (1914), 23

immunities, 69
impressing, 23
Incumbered Estates Court, 44
incumbrances, 47
industrial relations, 48
industrial schools, 55, 88
infanticide, 85n
inheritance laws, 68
Inn of Court of Northern Ireland, 58, 92
Inns of Court *see* King's Inns; London Inns
insanity, 29
insurance, 19, 49
Irish Academic Press, 102
Irish Archaeological Society, 13
Irish Commission (1622), 65n
Irish Convention (1917–1918), 20, 21
Irish Court of Admiralty *see* admiralty court
Irish Economic and Social History, 35
Irish Free State, 22, 38, 41, 44, 76, 77–8, 83, 84n, 90 *see also* Constitution of the Irish Free State, 1922
Irish Geography, 82
Irish Heritage Council, 62
Irish Historical Studies, 35, 39
Irish House of Commons, 39, 78
Irish House of Lords, 43, 78, 79
Irish independence, 19, 44, 73–4
Irish Jurist, 35
Irish Labour History Society, 35, 48
Irish Land Commission, 82
Irish language, 72
Irish law *see* early Irish law

Irish Legal History Society, 35, 85, 101–4
  inaugural lecture by W.N. Osborough (1988), 96–100
Irish Manuscripts Commission, 57, 65, 69, 70, 72
Irish nationalism, 31, 34
Irish neutrality, 78
Irish parliament, 15, 20–1, 26, 31, 39–41, 43, 78–9, 99 *see also* Dáil Éireann
  parliamentary register, 64, 78
  statutes, 63, 64 see also legislation
Irish privy council, 79
Irish Sailors' and Soldiers' Land Trust, 76n, 83

Jacobean period, 16, 31, 74
Jacobites, 26, 52
James I, king, 31, 43, 74
  directions of 1622, 25, 37
James II, king, 57, 74, 75, 91, 99
Jesuits, 41–2
Johnston, W.J., 13
Jones, Sir Edward, lord justice, 61
Journal of the Royal Society of Antiquaries, 35
Joyce, James, 73
Judicial Committee of the Privy Council, 44
judicial dress, 90
judicial reforms, 17
judicial review, 86
judiciary, 30, 60, 89–90, 100
  biographies, 59–61, 89
jury trial, 28, 49, 71, 73
jury-packing, 28
justices of the peace, 27

Keating, John, 89
Kelly, John, 92
Kennedy, Hugh, 61
Kennedy, Tristram, 56
Kenny, Colum, 102
Kerry bonds, 80
Kerry palatinate, 71
Kilmainham jail, Dublin, 29
Kilroy, Thomas, 84

Kilwarden, Viscount, 86
king's bench, court of, 23, 24, 51, 60, 72
King's Inns, Dublin, 32, 55–6, 57–8, 63, 91, 92n
kinship law, 68, 69
Knox v. Gavan (1836), 23
Kohn, Leo, 31

labour law, 28, 48–9, 84
Land Act, 1903, 47
land law, 27, 46–7, 82–3
Land War, 29, 47, 82
Landed Estates Court, 44, 47
landlord and tenant, 46–7
Larkin, John, 102
law reporting, 15, 16, 23, 27, 45, 63, 65, 79–80, 82, 85, 93–4
Law Society of Ireland, 56n, 57, 63
Law Society of Northern Ireland, 92n
law tracts, 66, 99
lawyers *see* legal profession
Lecky, W.E.H., 13
Lefroy, Thomas Langlois, 100
legal bibliography *see* bibliography
legal education, 32, 34, 56, 58, 92–3
legal profession, 31–2, 55–8, 68, 80, 90–3 *see also* recusant lawyers
  Catholics and, 31, 57, 91
  women in, 56–7, 58, 92
legal publishing, 32, 62–4, 93–4, 98–9, 102
legal writing, 62–4
Leggett v. Irish Sailors' and Soldiers' Land Trust (1932–33), 83
legislation, 20, 32n, 49, 63, 71, 77, 78–9, 82 *see also* Act of Union; penal laws; Poynings' Law
  publication of Irish statutes, 32n, 63, 64
Letterfrack Industrial School, 88n
Lex innocentium, 67n
libraries, 91
Limerick, 42, 71, 86n, 89, 91
Lisburn, Co. Antrim, 85
litigation, 33, 43
local courts, 80–1
local government, 42, 81

London, 26, 91
London Inns, 31, 58, 91n
Lough Neagh, 98
Loughgall, Co. Armagh, 93
Louth, county, 87
Lowry, Lord, 60, 61n, 96
Lowther, Gerard, lord chief justice, 38
Luddites, 48
lunatic asylums, 46
Lurgan, Co. Armagh, 93
Lutterell, Thomas, 71
Lutterellston, Co. Dublin, 71
Lynch, William, 99
Lyndhurst, Lord, 17n

MacCarwell, David, archbishop of Cashel, 69
MacDermott, John, lord chief justice, 60, 61
McKenna, John, 88n
Macnaghten, Lord, 60
MacNamara, Brinsley, 83
MacNeill, Eoin, 13
Magdalen laundries, 88
Magee, John, 72
Magee trials, 86–7
magistrates' courts, 27, 86
Magna Carta, 33
Mahon, Major, 87n
Maitland, Frederic, 103
malicious injuries code, 28
Mallon, Inspector, 88n
Malton, James, 93
manor courts, 26–7, 43–4
maritime jurisdiction *see* admiralty court
Marlay, Thomas, chief baron, 60, 89
marriage law, 28, 68
Marsh, Narcissus, 72, 79
Marsh's Library, Dublin, 72, 79
martial law, 41, 71, 74, 86
Mayne, Blair, 92
Maynooth Studies in Local History, 80, 82, 87
Meath, county, 69
Meath, earl of, 80
medicine, 85

medieval period, 15–17, 26–7, 28, 32, 36, 45, 46, 55, 69–70, 80, 97, 99
  see also early medieval period
mercy, prerogative of, 85, 86
Mervyn, Audley, 57
Mey, John, archbishop of Armagh, 70
Midland Health Board, In re (1988), 98n
Midleton, Viscount, 89
military establishment, 21
Milling, J.C., 61
minor offences, 28
Molony, Denis, 91
Molony, Sir Thomas, 61
Molyneux, William, 21, 41, 64, 74
Monaghan, county, 87
monasticism, 68
moral reform, 53
Morris, Lord, 60
mother and baby homes, 88
Mountjoy Prison, Dublin, 54
Mourne National Park
  proposal for, 82
Mulgrave, earl of, 17n
Mullet peninsula, Co. Mayo, 46–7
Munster presidency, 25, 30, 71–2
murder trials, 73, 85–6, 87

Nagle, Richard, 57
National Archives, 85
National Library of Scotland, 56
national parks, 82
national schools, 28
Navigation Acts, 80
Neale v. Cottingham (1770), 23
New Ross, Co. Wexford, 81
New South Wales, Australia, 54n
Newark, F.H., 14
Newfoundland, 23
Nine Years War (1594–1603), 16, 36
Norbury, Lord, 86
Northern Ireland, 19, 22, 52, 58, 61, 77, 82, 92
Northern Ireland Legal Quarterly, 92
Northern Law Club, 92
NUI Galway, 93

oaths, 40, 71
Ó Bruadair, Dáibhí, 89–90
O'Connell, Daniel, 32, 51, 86–7, 100
O'Connor, Sir James, 61
O'Curry, Eugene, 99
Ó Dálaigh, Cearbhall, 22
O'Davorens' law school, 66n
O'Doherty, Cahir, 43n
O'Donnell, Rory, 16
O'Donovan, John, 99
O'Hagan, Thomas, baron, 30, 60
O'Higgins, Paul, 92
O'Keeffe, Revd, 46
O'Keeffe v. Cardinal Cullen (1873), 23, 46n, 84
Old English, 15, 16, 18, 21
O'Malley, Ernie, 55
O'Neill, Hugh, 16
Oregan, Stephen, 97
O'Reilly, W.J., 61
Ormond palatinate (Tipperary), 26, 70–1
Ormonde, 2nd duke of, 26
O'Rourke, Brian, 50–1
Orpen, G.H., 13
Osborough, W.N.
  inaugural lecture to ILHS (1988), 96–100
  tribute to, 101–4
O'Sullivan, Daniel, 27
Ouzel Galley Society, 84

palatinate courts, 26
Pale, the, 36
Pale lawyers, 31
Palles, Christopher, 30
papal judges delegate, 46
parliamentary history *see* Irish parliament
parliamentary papers, 19, 64, 78, 85
Parnell, Charles Stewart, 30, 76
partition of Ireland, 21, 58, 76n
Party Procession Acts, 41
passport controversy (1923–24), 41
pastoral care, 68
Patriot Parliament (1689), 99
peace commission, 18
penal laws, 18, 20, 28, 40, 75, 76

penal reform, 54
penal system, 29, 54, 87–8
penitentials, 68
performing rights, 84
Perrot, Sir John, 86
Petty, Sir William, 43n, 60
petty sessions courts, 90
Pilgrim's Progress, 95
Plunket, Lord William Conyngham, 60
policing, 29–30, 52, 53–4, 88
political violence, 52–3 *see also* agrarian unrest
politics, 28, 29, 31, 39–40, 42, 52–3, 57, 59, 91, 100
Ponsonby, George, 73
poor law, 42
Popery laws, 80
Popish plot, 75
post-medieval legal system, 70–4
Powell, John Blake, 31
Poynings' Law, 1495, 39, 65, 75
Prene, John, archbishop of Armagh, 70
Prerogative and Faculties, court of, 45, 59
prerogative jurisdiction, 24, 25, 42
prerogative of mercy, 85, 86
presidency courts, 25, 30, 71
presidency of Republic of Ireland, 22
press freedom, 20
press regulation, 75
Presses Universitaires de Caen, 64
press-gang, 23
Prison Rules, 88
prison ships, 55
prison system, 29, 54–5, 87, 88
prisoners, 51
privy council, 44, 76n *see also* Irish privy council
prize, jurisdiction in, 26
procedure, 15, 18, 19, 22, 28, 49, 67n, 68, 80, 86
Proceedings of the Royal Irish Academy, 35
property law, 19, 27, 46–7
prostitution, 88n
Protectorate, 37

Protestants, 40, 43, 50n, 53, 59n *see also* Church of Ireland
proxies, 45
psychiatric hospitals, 88
public administration, 29–30
public dancing, 41
Public Record Office *see* Four Courts
publishing, 32, 35, 62–4

Queen's Bench, court of, 100
Queen's University, Belfast, 14, 22n, 47, 101, 103
quiet possession, 25
quominus, 80

R. (Martin) v. Mahony (1910), 86
Radcliffe, Sir George, 38
rape, 53
Rattigan, Terence, 58
Rea, John, 92
rebellion of 1641, 37
rebellion of 1798, 37, 39, 57, 86
recusant lawyers, 31, 57, 90
Redesdale, Lord, 93
Reeves, John, 14
Reformation, 43n, 46
reformation parliaments, 31
reformatories, 54, 88
Regan, John M., 88n
religion, 22, 27–8, 50n, 53, 79n, 90–1 *see also* church; ecclesiastical law
religious orders, dissolution of, 31
Republic of Ireland, 19, 22
republican courts *see* Dáil courts
republicans, 52, 87n
resident magistrates, 44, 61
Restoration period, 21, 37, 60n, 65, 74, 75n, 91
revenue police, 30
Rex v. Casement (1917), 86n
Ribbonism, 87n
Richmond penitentiary, 54
Ridgeway, William, 30
rights of way, 47
Roman Catholics *see* Catholics
Roscommon, county, 87
Rottrell, Sir George, 76n

Royal Hospital Kilmainham, In re (1966), 21n, 33
Royal Irish Academy, 35, 60
Royal Irish Constabulary, 30, 54, 88
Royal Society of Antiquaries, 35
Royal Ulster Constabulary, 88n
rural land distribution, 82
rural unrest, 52
Russell, Lord, 60

safety, health and welfare at work, 84
St Leger, Baron, 89
St Patrick's, Dublin, 80
St Sepulchre's, Dublin, 80
Sampson, William, 30
Santry, Henry, baron, 50
Saothar, 48
School of Celtic Studies, Dublin, 66
Scotland, 56, 96, 97
Scott, Sir Walter, 98
scutage, 69
secret societies, 30
secretary of state for Ireland, office of, 74
Selden, John, 96
Selden Society, 79–80, 89, 93–4, 96–7, 101, 103
Select Committee on Legal Education, 1846, 56n
Selwyn, ex parte (1872), 23
Senchas Már, 36n, 67n, 68
serjeants at law, 56n, 57
Sexton, Christopher, 91
Shaw, George Bernard, 77n
sheriffs, 15, 17, 18, 73
Singleton, Henry, 79, 89
Singleton Collection (Columbia University), 93
Sinn Féin, 44, 73–4
Slane manor, Co. Meath, 69
Slanes, Co. Down, 96
smuggling, 52
socage, 69
social control, 53
social reform, 29
social welfare, 78
solicitors (attorneys), 56, 57–8, 61, 92
  see also legal profession

Spanish Armada, 26
Special Criminal Court, 81
Stair, Viscount, 96
Stair Society, 96–7, 101
Stamp Act crisis (1760s), 75
Stannard, Eaton, 89
star chamber, 25
State Papers, 64, 70
statute law *see* legislation
statute staples, 49
Statutes of Kilkenny, 1366, 13
Stillingfleet, Edward, bishop of Worcester, 72
Stoker, Bram, 90n
Stormont, 22
Strokestown, Co. Roscommon, 87n
Stuart period, 24
substantive law, 27–9, 45–55
Supreme Court, 86
  'one-judgment' rule, 45
suretyship, 66
'surrender and regrant' policy, 15
Sutton Hoo, East Anglia, 97
Swayne, John, archbishop of Armagh, 70
Sweteman, Milo, archbishop of Armagh, 46, 70
Swift, Jonathan, 89
Sydney, Henry, 42

tanistry, 36
Thurneysen, R., 13
Tipperary, county, 48, 52
Tipperary palatinate, 26, 70–1
tithes, 17–18, 45, 52, 72
tolls and customs, 81
Toome Eel Co. (N. Ireland) Ltd v. Cardwell (1963), 33, 98n
tort law, 48
tracts, doctrine of, 36n
trade unions, 84
Traveller community, 88n
trials, 32, 49, 81, 85–7 *see also* jury trial
Trinity College Dublin, 32, 91, 92, 102
Trollope, Anthony, 56n
Truck Acts, 48

Tudor period, 15, 24, 35–6, 55, 64, 67n, 70–2, 74
Tuite, Fr., 84

Ulster, 16, 21, 25, 46, 49, 52, 53, 62, 85 *see also* Northern Ireland
Ulster Architectural Heritage Society, 62
Ulster Plantation, 16–17
unemployment insurance, 48–9
University College Dublin, 93, 102, 103
University College Galway, 93
university law schools, 92–3
urban protest, 87

vagrancy, 28, 71
The valley of the squinting windows (MacNamara), 83–4

Wainwright, Baron, 89
Wales, 68, 72
Walsh, Nicholas, 89–90
Wandesford, Christopher, 45n
wards and liveries, court of, 24
wardship, 24
Warwick, earl of, 59
Waterford, 81
Waters, Samuel, 54n
Webb v. Ireland (1988), 98n

Weldon v. Tuite, 84
Wentworth, Thomas, earl of Strafford, 18, 38, 42, 43
White Book of the Exchequer, 69
Whiteboys, 52
Wicklow Gaol, 87n
Wildgoose Lodge, Co. Louth, 52, 87
Willes, Edward, chief baron, 59
Willes, James Shaw, 30
William and Mary, 91
William III, king, 75
Williamite confiscation, 27
wills, 45n
The Winslow Boy (Rattigan), 58
witches, persecution of, 51
Wogan, John, 97
women, 28, 41, 67n, 78
    factory inspectors, 48
    in legal profession, 56–7, 58, 92
    litigants in chancery, 43
    police, 88
    teachers, 84
Wood, Herbert, 13, 14, 94
Wright v. Fitzgerald (1798), 23
Wylie, William Evelyn, 61, 89
Wyndham, Thomas, baron, 89

Youghal, Co. Cork, 97
Young Irelanders, 53
young offenders, 29

Irish Legal History Society

Established in 1988 to encourage the study and advance the knowledge of the history of Irish law, especially by the publication of original documents and of works relating to the history of Irish law, including its institutions, doctrines and personalities, and the reprinting or editing of works of sufficient rarity or importance.

PATRONS 2011–12

The Rt Hon. Sir Declan Morgan
Lord Chief Justice of Northern Ireland

The Hon. Mrs Justice Susan Denham
Chief Justice of Ireland

COUNCIL 2011–12

President
Professor Norma Dawson

Vice-Presidents
The Hon. Sir Donnell Deeny   Robert D. Marshall

Honorary Secretaries
Dr Niamh Howlin   Dr Thomas Mohr

Honorary Treasurers
John G. Gordon, esq.   Felix M. Larkin, esq.

Council Members

Ex Officio James I. McGuire, esq., President 2006–2009

Dr Kevin Costello
Dr Kenneth Ferguson
Dr Patrick Geoghegan
The Hon. Sir Anthony Hart
Daire Hogan, esq.
John Larkin QC
Yvonne Mullen BL

Dr Sean Donlan
The Hon. Hugh Geoghegan
Professor Desmond Greer QC (hon.)
Dr Robin Hickey
Professor Colum Kenny
His Honour John Martin QC
Professor Jane Ohlmeyer

www.ilhs.eu